The Development Officer in Higher Education:
Toward an Understanding of the Role

by Michael J. Worth and James W. Asp II

ASHE-ERIC Higher Education Report No. 4, 1994

D0792969

Prepared by

Clearinghouse on Higher Education
The George Washington University

In cooperation with

Association for the Study
of Higher Education

Published by

Graduate School of Education and Human Development
The George Washington University

Jonathan D. Fife, Series Editor

Cite as

Worth, Michael J., and James W. Asp II. 1994. *The Development Officer in Higher Education: Toward an Understanding of the Role.* ASHE-ERIC Higher Education Report No. 4. Washington, D.C.: The George Washington University, Graduate School of Education and Human Development.

Library of Congress Catalog Card Number 95-79710
ISSN 0884-0040
ISBN 1-878380-60-5

Managing Editor: Bryan Hollister
Manuscript Editor: Alexandra Rockey
Cover design by Michael David Brown, Rockville, Maryland

The ERIC Clearinghouse on Higher Education invites individuals to submit proposals for writing monographs for the *ASHE-ERIC Higher Education Report* series. Proposals must include:
1. A detailed manuscript proposal of not more than five pages.
2. A chapter-by-chapter outline.
3. A 75-word summary to be used by several review committees for the initial screening and rating of each proposal.
4. A vita and a writing sample.

ERIC **Clearinghouse on Higher Education**
Graduate School of Education and Human Development
The George Washington University
One Dupont Circle, Suite 630
Washington, DC 20036-1183

This publication was prepared partially with funding from the Office of Educational Research and Improvement, U.S. Department of Education, under contract no. ED RR-93-0200. The opinions expressed in this report do not necessarily reflect the positions or policies of OERI or the Department.

EXECUTIVE SUMMARY

Fund-raising has been a part of American higher education since its earliest days. In recent decades, however, it has become a central activity of most colleges and universities and the development officer has become an increasingly important figure in the administration of the institution. Despite its prominence, however, the role of the development officer is not well-defined or understood. The literature is often ambiguous or inconsistent concerning the development officer's proper role.

Major authors in the field can be placed into schools of thought depending upon which of four development-officer roles they advocate as most important. Authors of the "Salesman" viewpoint emphasize the development officer's activity as a solicitor of gifts; "Catalyst" authors view the development officer as working behind the scenes to support the fund-raising activities of presidents and volunteers; authors in the "Manager" category discuss the development officer's internal role in organizing fund-raising programs and staff; and some see the development officer playing the role of institutional "Leader," with a voice in policy decisions beyond fund-raising.

This report proposes a "development officer paradigm" that depicts the relationships among these four roles. This model includes two "vectors," one describing internal and the other external development functions. These vectors overlap, depending on the size of the particular development program. This paradigm provides a model for understanding and integrating the literature, for analyzing the staffing needs of a development office, for planning the progression of an individual development career, and for considering the major questions facing the development field.

What Personality Traits Are Required for Success as a Development Officer?

Authors who focus on the Salesman and Leader roles emphasize interpersonal skills and personal charisma. Those who focus on the development officer's role as a Catalyst or Manager more often emphasize the need for him or her to stay behind the scenes, remain anonymous, and "fit in" to the institutional culture.

Is Development an Art or a Science?

The literature provides muddled answers to this question, but authors of the Salesman and Leader points of view more often describe development as an art related to the development officer's inherent qualities and judgments. Those who favor the Catalyst and Manager roles more often discuss technical skills that can be taught and learned.

What Is the Appropriate Motivation for Entering a Development Career?

Some authors view development as a "calling" to be undertaken because of a deep commitment to philanthropy or an institution, often motivated by religious belief. Others are less inspirational in their tone, presenting development merely as a career field.

Is Development a "Profession"?

There is a consensus that development is not a mature profession, like medicine or law, but perhaps an emerging profession. Some writers express concern that development's advancement as a profession not lead its practitioners to become arrogant or alienated from their institutions.

What Should Be the Development Officer's Relationship to the President?

Authors who see the development officer as a Salesman, operating independently, tend to deemphasize the importance of other players. Most writers discuss a "fund-raising team" in which the president, trustees, and development officer all are important. The development officer's relationship to the president is especially critical and must be based on good personal chemistry as well as a common understanding of their respective roles.

What Should Be the Development Officer's Relationship to the Trustees?

Fund-raising is the one area in which trustees go beyond policy-making to play active roles. For this reason, the development officer is often closer to the trustees than anyone else on campus except the president. Most authors see the development officer in a Catalyst or Manager role with regard to the trustees and emphasize the need for appropriate boundaries to the development officer's influence with the board.

What Should Be the Development Officer's Role in Institutional Planning?

The literature is divided on this point. Some authors argue that development goals should be based on institutional priorities determined only by academic leaders. Others, particularly those who view the development officer as an institutional Leader, say that he or she should be involved in institutional planning. Research indicates that some development officers play this wider role.

Who Should Solicit the Gift?

Adherents to the Salesman perspective argue that the solicitation of gifts is too important to leave to amateurs and is best undertaken by professional development officers. Some authors of the Leader school agree. Those who see the development officer role as that of Catalyst or Manager say that the president and volunteers should solicit gifts, with the development staff playing behind-the-scenes support roles.

What Additional Research and Discussion Are Needed?

There is a need for more research and discussion regarding the development officer's role. A better understanding is needed of how development officers divide their time among the various roles, how institutional differences affect the roles development officers play, and how the styles and preferences of individual presidents and development officers can be identified and measured to create better working relationships.

What Is the Future of the Development Officer's Role?

Questions about the development officer's role in the future are related to declining volunteer involvement, the growing importance of planned giving, and the increasing complexity of development administrative operations. The development officer's role will likely change and evolve, as it has throughout the history of American higher education, in response to the changing needs of colleges and universities.

CONTENTS

FOREWORD

In 1990, we published a report by Brittingham and Pezzullo titled *The Campus Green: Fund Raising in Higher Education*. In the report, the theory of fund-raising, including donor behavior and motivation and the considerations of ethics and values in fund-raising, were reviewed. What was not covered in the analysis was a review of the professional role that can and should be performed by the development officer.

As the position of development officers has increasingly become commonplace—not only at the vice-president level but also at the individual school, college, and department level—it is necessary to develop a clear concept of the duties, responsibilities, and possibilities of this position. The role of the development officer has expanded to a level of significance whereby institutions no longer can afford to treat the position casually or as if someone with a minimal amount of training could fulfill the requirements.

A review of position notices for development officers found in the *Chronicle of Higher Education* illustrates the skills and responsibilities required. For example:

Master's degree. Experience interacting with the business community, promoting and handling fund-raising programs in a university setting. Excellent oral, written, and interpersonal communication skills. Strong organizational skills with knowledge of prospect identification, prospect donor research, cultivation, solicitation, and stewardship activities.

The successful candidate should have at least five years of development experience, preferably in managing aspects of annual giving programs in a large, urban research university. Thorough knowledge of state-of-the-art direct-mail and telemarketing operations is desirable. Bachelor's degree is required; graduate degree preferred.

These two positions are at the school or specific program level. At the vice-president level, the expectations are even more extensive:

Direct experience in the management of an annual gift-giving campaign, planned giving, major gifts, class reunions, capital campaigns, and corporate foundation solicitation is highly desirable. The vice president also will have proven experience with setting up and managing a donor research and tracking system, as well as coordinating the efforts of large groups of volunteers. The successful candidate should be an experienced development professional with at least five years of more progressively complex duties, of which three were in a senior administrative position. A proven track record in the field of higher education development or a closely related not-for-profit organization is preferred. The knowledge and ability to deal with legislative bodies and government agencies is desirable. The ability to think strategically and develop plans as well as to work directly with prospects.

The expectations for the development officer become clear when examining such solicitations. The fundamental questions are: Where do candidates for these positions receive their training? Is such training entirely on-the-job? Is there a framework that will define the role of development officers that can be used to create a base of professionalism for this position?

In this report by Michael J. Worth, vice president for development and alumni affairs and professor of education at The George Washington University, and James W. Asp II, associate vice president for university advancement at the University of California, Irvine, the development function in higher education is reviewed and the role of development officers is examined. The authors, through an analysis of the literature, develop a development-officer paradigm that structures several basic philosophical issues concerning the position of the development officer. The conclusions and recommendations of the authors help to define the professional role that this position plays in the higher education organization and set a foundation for formal programs for the training and professionalization of the development officer.

Jonathan D. Fife
Series Editor, Professor of Higher Education
Administration and
Director, ERIC Clearinghouse on Higher Education

ACKNOWLEDGMENTS

The authors acknowledge with gratitude the various scholars and practitioners upon whose work this volume draws. Their thoughtful consideration of issues in educational fund-raising has contributed to the status and effectiveness of the development field today. The authors also acknowledge with thanks the reviewers, whose comments were helpful, and ASHE-ERIC Series Editor Jonathan Fife, for his assistance and support. JWA expresses particular appreciation to Helen Lowe, who is responsible for his entrance into the development profession. MJW thanks his wife, Christine, for her support of this project.

INTRODUCTION

The pursuit of philanthropic support has been a part of American higher education from its beginning, and it has been an organized activity since at least the early part of the 20th century. Development officers, who are responsible for fund-raising, have become increasingly common fixtures of college and university administrative staffs in the years since World War II, as fund-raising has become a continuous activity and private gifts an increasingly important source of revenue for both private and public institutions. During the last two decades, the competitive environment of higher education has greatly increased the prominence of such individuals on American campuses as fund-raising goals and the resources devoted to achieving them have grown exponentially.

The chief development officer has an influence on overall policy beyond the scope of his or her specific responsibilities.

Development now is a substantial enterprise at many institutions, commanding large staffs and budgets. The chief development officer of a college or university often is a senior officer of the institution, reporting directly to the president with a place in the administrative hierarchy equivalent to that of academic, student, and business affairs. By virtue of this position as a member of top administration, the chief development officer has an influence on overall policy beyond the scope of his or her specific responsibilities. In a growing number of cases, development even has become a route to the college or university presidency. While development once may have been peripheral to the institution's mission and principal activities, its more central presence today cannot be ignored.

However, despite this growth in the scope and importance of the campus development officer's role, it remains relatively unexamined and the subject of differing perceptions. These differing perceptions are held by faculty members, presidents, trustees, and other volunteer leaders; even "chief development officers [themselves] . . . vary in how they conceptualize and carry out their multiple roles" (Duronio and Loessin 1991b, p. 208).

Because other administrative functions have been represented in the senior ranks of administration longer, they have been the subject of various studies and analyses. The development officer as a significant player in colleges and universities is a relatively recent phenomenon, and there has been little objective research concerning it. The literature on the subject largely reflects the experiences and opinions of various authors.

For these reasons, this report differs somewhat from typical reviews which attempt to synthesize the literature and distill the consensus of research. Because there is little research and not a clear consensus, this report is not an analysis of the development officer's role based on the literature so much as it is an analysis of the literature itself. It does not seek to establish a unifying "theory" but merely to clarify the issues raised by the literature as a starting point for needed further examination. The authors will be pleased if this modest objective is achieved.

This report identifies four "schools of thought" or, more precisely, "habits of thought" concerning the development officer's role. These schools are not distinct and the positions of various authors within them are not always stated explicitly; they must be discerned from the biases and nuances in their words—by what they do not address as well as by what they do. Therefore, this report quotes extensively. With recognition of the difficulty this may present for the casual reader, the authors believe it to be essential to their purpose. Additionally, because the literature consists largely of opinion and perception rather than objectively determined truth, it is often necessary to identify the authors by their professional positions to develop an understanding of their points of view.

Following an introductory chapter that reviews the history and current status of the development function, major authors on the subject are reviewed and placed into the four "schools of thought." A paradigm is offered as a model for analyzing the development officer role and the literature concerning it. Again, this falls far short of a "theory" and is intended only as a conceptual and visual tool for further thinking and research.

Finally, this report examines eight questions—four that are characterized as "philosophical" and four others deemed "practical." Generally, authors' opinions on these questions reflect their leanings among the four schools of thought previously identified.

We believe that the role of the development officer in higher education today warrants more discussion and more research than it has previously received. Development has found its place in the administration of colleges and universities; it should be equally prominent in the interests of scholars who study higher education and its institutions. Several avenues for such further investigation are suggested in the concluding chapter of this volume.

THE DEVELOPMENT FUNCTION IN HIGHER EDUCATION

The American system of higher education is unique in the world. It is generally acknowledged as the best, and it also provides an unmatched degree of institutional diversity and freedom. In most nations, colleges and universities are controlled by the state. In the United States, however, the earliest colleges were established independently, often by churches, and were funded primarily through private resources. This beginning established a tradition of private initiative and competition among institutions that survived even the establishment of our public universities in the 19th and 20th centuries.

Public universities in the United States were influenced by the model of the private institutions that preceded them. Rather than being controlled directly by the state, they are governed by relatively independent boards of regents or trustees. While politically appointed or elected, these boards nevertheless provide a buffer between the institution and the power of government. This freedom enables them to compete with other institutions for students, status, and resources, including private as well as public funds.

It is this element of competition among institutions that distinguishes the American system of higher education and results in its diversity and quality. Competition fosters initiative and innovation, leading to excellence. And in no area is the competition more intense than in the quest for private gift dollars with which to support educational and research programs, build and improve campus facilities, and secure the financial base through the growth of endowment funds.

In this light, it is not surprising that from the beginning the pursuit of gifts has been an important part of American higher education. Nor is it surprising that in the intensely competitive environment of the late 20th century, the fund-raising or "development" enterprise has become a substantial aspect of American higher education. Today, most every college or university employs a director of development or a vice president for development among its key administrative officers. In many institutions the development operation represents a substantial commitment of resources. College and university campaigns, seeking hundreds of millions of dollars, and in a few cases billions of dollars, have become the subject of discussion in the popular media as well as higher education circles.

Today, the chief development officer of a college or university usually sits alongside the chief academic officer and the chief financial officer at the president's cabinet table and has a voice in matters of institutional policy. Despite the importance of the development function and the key role played by the development officer in today's college or university, considerable ambiguity exists concerning his or her proper role and responsibilities. Written principally by professional consultants and institutional practitioners in the field, the literature reveals varied perceptions of the development officer's role and even a lack of agreement on the terms by which the field is identified.

Development and Fund-Raising

The term "development" is most commonly used interchangeably with "fund-raising" today. However, the use of the term "development" originated at Northwestern University in the 1920s and had a broad meaning that encompassed a variety of institutional objectives, including building acceptance for the institution, recruiting students, and obtaining financial support.

> *The period just after the first World War was a time of decision for Northwestern. . . . [T]he University had to decide whether to remain what it was or to become a great university in the modern sense. It chose the latter course.*

> *Although the first step in this new direction was the launching of a bold campaign to create a skyscraper metropolitan campus to house the professional schools, the people behind the undertaking realized that greatness would never result from this short-term project alone. They realized that the decision to move forward carried with it an indefinite commitment to the future.*

> *A special department of the university was created to serve in meeting this commitment. . . . [S]omewhere in the course of discussions and committee meetings, the phrase "Department of Development" was coined* (Stuhr 1977, pp. 3-4).

Over the years, however, the term "development" came to have a narrower meaning, synonymous with "fund-raising," while the term "institutional advancement" has been widely accepted as the common designation for the wider range of functions. Institutional advancement is usually defined to include alumni relations, public relations and communications, and development or fund-raising. Student recruitment, or "enrollment management," and government relations sometimes also are included.

For simplicity, this report follows the contemporary practice and uses the terms "development" and "fund-raising" interchangeably. However, some writers insist that the distinction is important. Worth states that "development is a sophisticated *process* that includes several steps or stages" (1993, p. 6). These steps include defining the institution's academic and financial needs, identifying potential donors to help meet those needs, cultivating the interest and involvement of these prospective donors in the life of the institution, matching their interests and desires with the needs and goals of the college or university, soliciting the gift, and stewardship to assure that the gift is properly applied and the donor kept informed. "Only when [the] initial steps in the development process have been achieved is the institution ready for fund raising, which in its narrowest sense means solicitation, or simply 'asking for gifts'" (Worth 1993, p. 7). Development and fund-raising are further distinguished, as are the roles of "development officer" and "fund-raiser," as follows:

> [F]und raising is but one aspect of a complex process involving the institution, its hopes and goals, and the aspirations of its benefactors. Fund raising is episodic; development is continuous. Fund raising is focused on a particular objective or set of goals; development is a generic and long-term commitment to the financial and physical growth of the institution. Successful fund raising requires a specific set of interpersonal and communicative skills; development requires a broader understanding of the institution and its mission as well as patience, judgment, and sensitivity in building relationships over the long haul. A "fund raiser" is an individual skillful in soliciting gifts; a "development officer" may be a fund raiser, but he or she is also a strategist and manager of the entire development process (Worth 1993, pp. 7-8).

Development is also viewed as more professional than fund-raising:

> Fund raising as a professional process is best understood when considered in the broader process "development." The

*latter term encompasses the entire operation from goal iden-
tification to gift solicitation. Fund raising should not be con-
fused with "tin cupping." Almost anyone can get token
donations. High school band members can sell candy to buy
new uniforms. What we are dealing with is the professional
process involved in securing significant support* (Broce
1979, p. 27).

And, Robert Payton writes that

*Properly understood, fund raising rises to its rightful role
as institutional development. The development function
integrates with the academic objectives of the institution.
It is as honorable and useful and important as any other
function in achieving institutional purposes* (1989, p. 35).

Greenfield gives an even more vaunted and sweeping definition, invoking the term "philanthropy in practice" to include
"incorporation, noble purpose, government endorsement,
legal structure, formal mission, voluntary leadership, and stewardship of funds, all of which are carried out openly" (1991,
p. 5).

Indeed, for some, the term "fund-raising" is viewed as so
insultingly narrow that " . . . to equate *development* with *fund
raising . . .* will outrage many who have struggled for years
to create a larger vision of the field" (Payton 1981, p. 282).

History of the Development Function
The first recorded fund-raising effort of an American college
occurred in 1641, when William Hibbens, Hugh Peter, and
Thomas Weld set sail from Boston to London on a mission
to solicit gifts for young Harvard College (Cutlip 1965).

Despite these early beginnings, fund-raising methods
throughout the 18th and 19th centuries were primitive by
today's standards, consisting mostly of "passing the church
plate, of staging church suppers or bazaars, and of writing
'begging letters'" (Cutlip 1965, p. 7). The "begging" usually
was performed by a trustee, the president, or a paid agent.
Paid agents were often given a percentage of the funds raised.

Because the early colleges were often connected with a
sponsoring church, their fund-raising reflected a religious zeal.
Gift solicitations were often based on the need to advance

Christianity in a young and uncivilized nation as well as other, purely charitable appeals. George Whitfield, a noted early fund-raiser for Harvard, Dartmouth, Princeton, and the University of Pennsylvania, combined his solicitations for higher education with fund-raising to help "the poor" (Cutlip 1965). Even the paid agents of colleges were often motivated primarily by their religious convictions. In addition to their fund-raising activities, many also played roles in the academic and business affairs of the colleges for which they solicited gifts. Thus, educational fund-raising in these early years was anything but professional and organized. It was a personal undertaking, and a gift was essentially a transaction between two individuals.

The first organized efforts were the alumni annual funds. Alumni interest and loyalty was evident from the earliest years of American institutions, and systematic solicitations for alumni gifts were undertaken beginning in the 1800s. But the most significant changes in fund-raising practices occurred in the early 20th century, and they originated outside of higher education.

> *The emergence of what historians have labeled the Progressive Movement at the turn of the century . . . began to produce fundamental changes among fund raisers. As social welfare and various public agencies proliferated in the epoch, the number of individuals involved in philanthropic activities likewise extended the purview of those citizens asked to contribute to these organizations. To reach more individuals, fund raisers (still amateurs at this point) were forced to create more innovative techniques* (Harrah-Conforth and Borsos 1991, p. 21).

In 1902, Lyman L. Pierce, a YMCA executive and fund-raiser, began a campaign to raise funds toward construction of a new YMCA in Washington, D.C. By 1905, the campaign was floundering short of its goal. Pierce called on Charles Sumner Ward, a fellow YMCA executive from Chicago who had gained attention for his fund-raising skills, to join him in Washington to help complete the campaign. The result was a revolution in fund-raising practice and the "invention" of the fund-raising "campaign."

> *The collaboration of Ward and Pierce produced the first modern fund-raising campaign techniques: careful organ-*

ization, picked leaders spurred on by team competition,
prestige leaders, powerful publicity, a large gift to be
matched . . . , careful records, report meetings, and a def-
inite time limit (Cutlip 1965, p. 44).

Although Pierce and Ward collaborated on this historic campaign, its procedures became generally known as the "Ward
method" of fund-raising. In 1914, the University of Pittsburgh
hired Ward to conduct a campaign, representing the first application of his methods to higher education. Ward recruited
others to work on the Pittsburgh campaign, including Carlton
and George Ketchum, Arnaud Marts, and others who later
became prominent names in educational fund-raising and
whose names still are associated with national consulting
firms they founded. Indeed, it was through their role as consultants to colleges and universities that Ward and his disci-
ples established their process as standard practice and the
campaign method as the principal fund-raising strategy for
colleges and universities.

Ward was the first to demonstrate that fund-raising success
depended as much on "method" as on the personalities of
the individuals involved. This emphasis on "method" represented a significant change from earlier fund-raising, which
rested primarily on the personal appeal of individual solicitors. For the first time, fund-raising was viewed as a systematic
activity, based on a body of knowledge, applied by a professional specialist. In his commitment to process, Ward was a
new type of "fund-raiser," a professional who set the strategy
and managed the overall enterprise but who was not himself
a solicitor of gifts. The gift solicitations were conducted by
volunteers and institutional leaders following Ward's professional direction.

One of Ward's associates, Carlton Ketchum, described Ward
as "an austere and reserved man, very far indeed from any
of the campaign types which we all know." Ward's effectiveness, Ketchum said, "was that of the originator of a sane and
practical method, and the firmness to insist on its thorough
application . . . rather than any personal magnetism" (Cutlip
1965, p. 86).

Consulting firms such as those founded by Ward and his
contemporaries directed most college and university fund-
raising campaigns in the first half of the 20th century. Following Ward's example, the consultant sent to a campus to man-

age the campaign, usually called the "resident manager," did not actually solicit gifts but guided the efforts of volunteers and institutional leaders and enforced their adherence to the campaign process. College and university campaigns were sporadic during this time, usually occurring once or twice in a decade for a concentrated period of about three years. Once the campaign ended, the consultant moved on to the next assignment; the institution's development program, except, perhaps, for the ongoing alumni fund, stopped until it was time to begin the next campaign.

As fund-raising pressures became more intense in the post-World War II era, institutional development programs became continuous efforts. This created a need for a permanent "expert" on the college or university staff and the position of "director of development" was created. The transition from occasional campaigns conducted by temporary consultants to ongoing programs managed by full-time staff professionals was gradual. A survey by the American College Public Relations Association in 1949 found only two members with the title "director of development." In 1952, another survey discovered only 13 (Pray 1981). Today, nearly every college and university has at least one and in many cases dozens of development professionals on the institutional staff. Consultants are still retained but more often to give targeted advice rather than to manage a campaign on a full-time basis.

The role of the college or university development officer thus originated in the for-profit consulting world. For the first half of the 20th century, the campus' fund-raising professional indeed came from outside the academic world and clearly was motivated more by the quest for personal gain than by loyalty to the institution. Even today, some development officers move back and forth from institutional positions to for-profit consulting roles. The legacy of this history may account, at least in part, for why there continues to be a perceived cultural gap between them and members of the academic community.

Development Today
In recent decades, the practice of development has continued to become increasingly professionalized. The number of institutions actively seeking gift support has increased, and development officers are now found at most state universities and community colleges as well as private institutions. And, they

have been called upon to meet ever-higher fund-raising goals, as philanthropy has become a vital source of revenue both for current operating budgets and capital growth.

To say that development has become more professionalized in its approach is not to say that it has yet become a true "profession," like medicine or law. That is a subject of debate, and it is more fully explored later in this report. But today's development officers have an established body of knowledge, based on experience as well as research, and fairly standard procedures—a far cry from the idiosyncratic and personality-based approach of the pre-Ward era discussed earlier. Recent years have seen the growth of a substantial professional literature, formalized training programs for development officers, and attempts at establishing a formal code of ethics. In earlier decades, development officers could learn their trade only through experience or the tutelage of a senior practitioner. Francis Pray describes his appointment to his first development position in the 1940s:

> *When the president of the small college I worked for asked me to 'take over the alumni fund,' I accepted with alacrity, almost instantly afterward realizing that I knew nothing about it, either specifically or generically* (1981, p. 2).

Today, programs offered by the Council for Advancement and Support of Education, the National Society of Fund-Raising Executives, and other organizations provide much more systematic training and have greatly improved the professionalism and skill of educational fund-raisers. The 1980s have even seen the initiation of degree programs in "institutional advancement," which includes development, at several universities and an increasing amount of scholarly research in the field.

As discussed above, the first colleges and universities in the United States were private institutions, and fund-raising played an important part in their survival and growth. State universities were established much later but followed the example of the private institutions in many aspects of their governance. The development function is, however, a relatively new part of the administration of public universities.

Some state universities, particularly those in the Midwest, engaged in fund-raising almost from their beginnings. For example, the Kansas University Endowment Association was established in 1891 to receive and manage gifts from alumni and friends of the university. But state universities in the East, which developed in the shadow of more-established private institutions, generally were not involved in raising funds from the private sector until the last 30 years. Many state institutions in the West started even later. Development staffs and budgets at public colleges and universities have grown dramatically in recent years, however, and they have narrowed the fund-raising gap with the private institutions.

Private support for public universities totaled just $356 million in 1971-72, representing 21.6 percent of the total $1.6 billion given to all of higher education. By the end of the 1980s, public institutions' share of all giving to higher education had reached $2.67 billion—nearly a third of the total (Council for Aid to Education 1990). This trend has moderated in the 1990s, however. In 1993, for the first time in more than a decade, public institutions failed to achieve larger increases in giving than their private counterparts (Council for Aid to Education 1994). The most rapidly growing fund-raising programs in recent years have been at community colleges, which doubled their gift support from $44 million in 1988-89 (Council for Aid to Education 1990) to $88 million in 1992-93 (Council for Aid to Education 1994).

In 1993, for the first time in more than a decade, public institutions failed to achieve larger increases in giving than their private counterparts.

Increased support of public institutions reflects the growth of their development programs, staffs, and budgets throughout the previous decade. A study in the early 1980s found that 67 percent of state universities had established private foundations for fund-raising purposes (Reilly 1985). A 1987 study found that the percentage having such foundations had increased to 86 percent (Worth 1989).

Today, there are few institutions—large or small, public or private—that do not employ at least one full-time development officer, and some large universities have development staff numbering in the hundreds. The Council for Advancement and Support of Education was established in 1974 through a merger of the American Alumni Council and the American College Public Relations Association. It includes development officers as well as professionals in the other institutional advancement specialties and has become the largest nonprofit educational association, with more than 14,400 members (Council for Advancement and Support of Education 1994).

The fund-raising goals of colleges and universities have

grown as quickly as their development staffs and budgets. Cutlip traces the growth of Harvard fund-raising in the 20th century through the goals of three campaigns: The campaign of 1904-05 had a goal of $2.5 million; a 1919-20 campaign raised more than $14 million; Harvard's 1956-60 campaign raised what Cutlip called "the staggering sum of $82,775,553" (1965, p. 480). Since the time of Cutlip's analysis, Harvard's campaign goals have continued their steep climb. In the spring of 1994, Harvard announced a campaign to raise $2.1 billion, six times the $358 million raised in its 1979-85 campaign (Blumenstyk 1994). Such dramatic increases have been seen at many other institutions as well.

Turnover, Image, and Acceptance
Despite its growth, increasing professionalization, and ever-more important place in colleges and universities, development is still striving to define itself as a field and continues to be troubled by problems of instability, image, and acceptance. In 1987, Edward G. Thomas conducted a study and found a 19.5 percent turnover rate among development officers in higher education: Of those who were working in the field at the start of 1986, nearly 20 percent had left their jobs, voluntarily or otherwise, by the end of the year. Looking elsewhere in higher education for comparisons, he found the rate to be 11.4 percent for student-affairs professionals and 9.9 percent for fiscal administrators. To provide broader perspective, Thomas compared this rate with that of office workers in several different types of organizations. Only the turnover rate for hourly employees, 19 percent, approached that of development officers. The rate for salaried workers in other fields was just 11 percent (Thomas 1987).

Thomas found that 19.4 percent of the turnover among development professionals was by those with less than a year of experience. This may explain the fact that the most common reason cited for voluntary turnover was "to take a higher-level position" (1987, p. 11). To some extent, maybe this is happy news—development has been an expanding profession through much of the last two decades, and people entering the field have found it relatively easy to move up quickly to higher-paying and more responsible positions. But some turnover is involuntary and some that is nominally voluntary reflects an underlying dissatisfaction. In any case, no matter what the implications for the individuals, it is difficult to believe that such turnover is anything but detrimental to the institutions, since fund-raising requires the establishment of relationships over a period of time.

The traditional view of faculty toward college and university fund-raisers has been suspicious and dismissive. To academics, development officers sometimes represent an image that is inconsistent with academic values, and fund-raising represents an intrusion of commercial values into the academy that is, at the least, uncomfortable. This traditional disdain perhaps has been somewhat ameliorated in recent years as the development field has attracted more people with advanced degrees and a more professional mode of operation. But, this increasing professionalism has given rise to a new line of criticism: that development professionals have become arrogant and self-important.

Charles Lawson, president of Brakeley John Price Jones Inc., one of the most prominent consulting firms in the field, criticizes those "who have become so consumed with the trappings of professionalism and personal advancement that the reason for serving philanthropic causes is largely forgotten." He charges that "professional egomania in the fund-raising field is rapidly growing beyond acceptable boundaries and its basis is largely unjustified" (1990, pp. 9-10).

It seems reasonable to assume a relationship between the field's struggle for stability and recognition and the absence of a common understanding on what the development officer's roles should be. This may be an outgrowth of the field's evolution over the course of American higher education, as previously discussed. But it remains a problem, limiting the full effectiveness of development officers and their contributions to the colleges and universities they serve.

Summary

Fund-raising has been a part of American higher education from the beginning, reflecting the competitive nature of colleges and universities in the United States. The term "development" is usually used interchangeably with "fund-raising" today, although it originally had a broader meaning and some writers continue to make a distinction between the two concepts.

Early college fund-raisers were principals in the institution, and some were paid agents who received a percentage of the funds raised. With the advent of the campaign method in the early 20th century, developed principally by Charles Sumner Ward, higher education fund-raising became more systematic, and the role of a development "professional" was created. Initially, these professionals were consultants who served colleges and universities from the for-profit sector, but with the growth of institutional programs this expertise was brought in-house and development officers were added to college and university staffs.

Development staffs and budgets have grown in recent years at private and public institutions, and the chief development officer is an important member of the senior staff at most colleges and universities. However, the field continues to be plagued by instability, including rapid turnover, and is viewed with disdain by some members of the academic community. These problems may be related to continuing ambiguity, reflected in the literature, concerning the development officer's proper role and responsibilities.

ROLES OF THE DEVELOPMENT OFFICER

The history of the development function reveals the evolution
of four distinct roles for the development officer. The earliest
figures were the paid agents, whose responsibility was limited
to the solicitation of gifts. With the advent of Charles Sumner
Ward and his method, a new role emerged—that of the facilitator or catalyst—a "fund-raiser" who did not solicit gifts but
directed the efforts of volunteers and institutional leaders
according to an established method.

As this professional function moved in-house with the
appointment of development officers to institutional staffs,
a third role was added: manager and administrator. As the
development officer assumed greater responsibilities and was
viewed as vital to the institution's financial health, more
resources were committed to the development staff and
budget.

Chief development officers today

*have become managers of large and complex offices and
consequently must build their own administrative staffs.
Thus the modern collegiate institution is operated by a large
administrative staff, and its key administrators, like those
in business and industry, can become detached from the
daily operation of the institution and its primary activity—
education* (Coloia 1980, p. 40).

A fourth addition to the development officer's responsibility
is the direct result of this increased significance of his or her
role: institutional leader. The quantitative increase in staff and
resources allotted to development has resulted in a qualitative
difference in the development officer's perceived role. The
chief development officer now is regarded by many as an
important participant in the articulation of the institution's
mission and purpose and the strategic planning undertaken
to achieve these ends. Fund-raising is now integral to institutional priorities. This is so not only because of the importance of the revenues generated but also because "each
accepted gift, with all its stipulations and restrictions, is a state-
ment about what the institution is willing to become [and]
how it is willing to see itself and the world" (Brittingham and
Pezzullo 1990, p. 57).

Historically, then, development officers (or, rather, their
antecedents) originally only were gift solicitors. Over time,

additional responsibilities were added: strategizer and imple-menter of the campaign method; in-house manager of the expanded development office staff; and, finally, institutional leader. This broad historical evolution is mirrored in the nar-rower growth of specific development offices in many insti-tutions. The careers of many individual development officers follow an analogous path: starting as the young and eager "annual fund worker"; undertaking some responsibility for organizing and staffing a small group of volunteer solicitors; being promoted to a position with managerial responsibilities; and finally, assuming a leadership role within the entire institution.

The four main historical accretions outlined above are reflected in today's development literature. On the surface, there is the appearance of disagreement among authors about which of them is the appropriate focus for a practicing devel-opment officer. Consider, for example, the different view of the development officer's role as described by prominent authors in the field. Jerold Panas recalls,

> *I was at a conference recently that covered, among others, these subjects: Writing a Case Statement, Development Soft-ware, Planned Giving Software, Successful Special Events, Employee Campaigns, and Marketing Planned Giving. Not one of these, not one, has anything to do with being a really successful fundraiser* (1988, p. 148).

Authors Robert Berendt and J. Richard Taft, writing to chief executive officers about the development professional's role, present a very different picture:

> Fund raisers . . . do not, by and large, raise money. *They do prospect research. They train volunteers. They write pro-posals. They prepare brochures. They set up record-keeping systems. All of which is part of the process of orchestrating the institution's management and leadership to participate in its visits to foundations, corporations, and individual donors* (1983, pp. 33-34, authors' emphasis added).

More often than not, however, authors writing about devel-opment do not state their views in explicit terms. Their assumptions about the development officer's proper role are implied by what they do or do not say, or by what they say in passing. For example, in an article dealing with staff training issues, Karen Osborne begins a case study as follows:

Jeff had just joined the development office. Every time I walked by his office, his head was bent over his desk, and he was either diligently writing or absorbed in reading. Because a good development officer spends most of the time speaking on the phone or traveling, *I was naturally concerned* (1993, p. 243, emphasis added).

As we will see below, what Osborne assumes regarding a development officer's proper activities is disputed by other writers in the field.

The following sections analyze the literature to determine the underlying assumptions of various authors and delineate "schools of thought." Many discussions of the development process acknowledge the roles of solicitor, volunteer trainer and supporter, administrative manager, and institutional leader. However, most authors emphasize one role, while neglecting another. Or they pay lip service to one aspect of the job, while relishing the discussion of the others.

The metaphors used by authors in the field often reveal a great deal about their underlying attitudes. This is so because "metaphors are central to our definitions of ourselves and to how a person presents herself or himself to others" (Turner 1991, p. 40). So, for example, the use of business or military metaphors, both common in fund-raising, say much about the writer's orientation toward the profession. As Richard Turner has written, "the presence of the metaphor suggests an orientation of values and perceptions of reality that are significant and worthy of comment" (1991, p. 38).

Therefore, individual prejudices, personal interests, and predilections often underlie the assumptions inherent in each publication. While reading these works, it is possible to determine to which parts of the development-officer job description the author is drawn.

For purposes of analysis, various viewpoints on the role of the development officer can be placed into four descriptive categories: the Salesman, the Catalyst, the Manager, and the Leader. These terms are not all-encompassing, and other terms may be as descriptive. But these categories do summarize the significant aspects of the development officer's job discussed in the literature. Those who have written of the development officer's role often cross over these categorical lines, so they are not completely discrete. However, they are helpful concepts to use to identify tendencies and similar habits of thought among the various authors.

The Salesman

Those authors who write from the Salesman perspective emphasize direct solicitation as the primary role for the development officer. For these authors, the development officer's job is simple to define: Go out and get the gift. Panas perhaps best exemplifies this view. He writes,

> *The most effective fundraisers, I find, are motivators—men and women who inspire others to give at the very highest level . . . Great fundraisers have the glorious capacity to touch the heart and set the stands roaring* (1988, pp. 93-4).

As discussed, many authors are careful to make a distinction between the definitions of the words "development" and "fund-raising." Harold (Sy) Seymour's definition often is cited: "The word 'development' . . . should not be taken merely as another word for raising money, but as a broad term for the planned promotion of understanding, participation, and support" (1966, p. 115).

Those who write from the perspective of the Salesman category, however, do not share this prejudice. Panas comments that,

> *There is a tendency these days in our profession to use euphemisms. It's been polished to an art. It's called marketing, investing, development, advancement—almost anything but fundraising. But fundraising is a high calling. And fundraising is really what it's all about* (1988, p. 63).

When discussing the solicitation process, those who subscribe to the Salesman approach think in terms of a business transaction. Panas advises,

> *The problem is that many fundraisers can't stop talking. Too often they forget the basic rule of selling: Find out what the customer wants, and give it to them. To be effective in this business, you have got to 'suspend your own agenda.' You must forget what you were going to say and try to sell, and listen to what your prospect wants to say* (1988, p. 147).

Invoking similar language, Warren Gould asks, "How can listening help us as fund raisers if we see our ultimate goal as that of a salesman? How can we listen carefully when we are programmed to sell?" (Koile and Gould 1981, p. 291). Among his characteristics of a successful fund-raiser, Gary Evans includes "a bottom-line orientation" and "eagerness to be measured. A professional in development welcomes specific goals and expects—even wants—to be measured by the success of achieving them" (1986, p. 247). J. Barry McGannon describes the process in terms of corporate sales: "Would IBM, or any major business, entrust its biggest customers to an amateur? Of course not. IBM wants more quality control than that, and so should we" (1992, p. 18).

Often, the Salesmen present the development job as a simple, personal, back-to-basics, "seat of the pants" occupation. The best development officers, then, are roll-up-the-sleeves characters. As Panas writes,

Just stay as close as you possibly can to your prospects, and keep in close enough contact that you know how they are feeling. What they are feeling. What is necessary to make them buy. You don't need market research and you don't need demographic information. Just stay close (1988, p. 151).

Authors in the Salesman category evoke images of the early college fund-raisers, loners who raise money based on their personal energy and charisma and with no need for any method or systematic approach.

The Catalyst
A number of different terms are used to describe this particular role of the development officer: sales manager, adviser, expert, facilitator. The word "Catalyst" is chosen here because it captures not only the description of what the development officer is believed to do but also the way in which it is done. Those who see the development officer's role as that of the Catalyst seem to understand its proactive nature, even as they maintain a certain distance between the development officer and the prospects. Just as the catalytic agent is not changed itself when it causes changes in other ingredients, so the development officer causes the solicitation but remains at arm's length from the actual process.

The role of the Catalyst was defined within the world of consulting, and it is not surprising that many of today's consultants define the development officer in these terms. Arthur Frantzreb refers to the development officer as a "sales manager" (Coloia 1980, p. 60) or, in more updated language, as "investment counselors for your organization's fiscal stability and security" (1991, p. 118). A number of years ago, he predicted, "[t]he words sales, goals, schedules, profits, market, testing, productivity and responsibility have been no-no's in the educational vocabulary too long. Not so in this decade" (1970, pp. 15-16).

Another prominent consultant, Robert Tinker, has written, "It is the responsibility of the development officer to keep reminding, prompting and urging trustees, the president, faculty, staff and even students of their responsibilities in the major gift effort" (Coloia 1980, p. 60).

George Brakeley Jr., like his fellow consultants, uses the words "planning, organizing, direction, control, and coordination" to describe the role of a vice president for development (1980, p. 61). All of these words suggest distance and some removal from the actual solicitation process. Seymour summarizes the Catalyst view as follows:

Most valuable of all, in the opinion of many wise laymen heard over a long period of time, is the function of the catalytic agent — seeing that the right things happen at the right time and that everything keeps rolling right along (1966, p. 173).

Seymour is writing specifically about the role of consultants, but his view extends to institutional development staff as well. However, Kathleen Kelly maintains that the roles of outside consultants and institutional staff are distinct. She notes that in many instances the latter do solicit gifts and she argues that the consultants' devotion to the catalyst model is explained by their own self-interests. She writes,

[T]he myth of the volunteer solicitor and its corollary, the myth of the invisible fund raiser, are primarily attributable to the historical evolution of the fund-raising function and to the self-interests of commercial fund-raising firms that do not solicit money as a part of their consulting service (1991, p. 18).

However, institutional development officers also use Catalyst terms in describing their roles. Kent Dove, for example, describes the development officer as "the catalytic force—an educator, manager, researcher, communicator, facilitator, leader, guide, and stimulator" (1988, p. 40). This perceived role also has been termed "enabling" (prior to the current, generally negative, connotation of that word):

The role of the development director tends to be that of a background person. . . . The director is an enabler—one who, realizing the paramount importance of the volunteers, enables them to perform their fund raising assignments with ease and dispatch. The director does not solicit, but prepares the way for the solicitor (Pendleton 1981, p. 8).

The fact that the development officer works with a group is critical in this view. A Salesman can be a kind of "lone wolf," operating alone, with minimal outside support or constraint, and therefore largely reliant upon personal abilities and traits. The Catalyst must be part of some organizational net.

In the view of these authors, "Fund raisers are often facilitators rather than solicitors; success is therefore a group achievement" (Payton, Rosso, and Tempel 1991b, p. 13). Henry Rosso emphasizes the need for "team building" both inside and outside the institution. Externally, the "[r]ecruitment of dedicated, supportive volunteers must start early and end late" while internally, "[t]he flag for fund raising must always fly from the flagpole of the board and the senior management offices, reminding everyone of the interrelatedness of responsible management, responsible programs, and productive fund raising" (1991, pp. 14+).

The Manager

Another group of authors focus much more intensely on the role of the development officer as manager or administrator. In most cases, they also outline other responsibilities, but their focus is on tasks associated with management, organization, and direction of internal resources. T.E. Broce, for example, includes among his characteristics of the successful fund-raiser the following:

Accepts responsibility, establishes standards, originates action, sustains a mood, and keeps things going. . . . Has

"Fund raisers are often facilitators rather than solicitors; success is therefore a group achievement."

the capability to coordinate special events to take maximum advantage of such occasions . . . Has the skills (or is acquiring them) to provide the mechanical and professional support necessary in all phases of the development process (1979, p. 42).

In many ways, the Manager approach is the opposite of the Salesman approach. For example, Greenfield describes the development officer's role thus:

There is more to fund-raising than asking for money. The development office must be managed so that all operations run smoothly throughout the year. Increased net proceeds, sound accounting procedures, and expert management of all funds raised will be the measurable evidence of the fund development professional's performance. . . . Success as a manager of fund development means success as a manager of the fund development office (1991, p. 191).

This understanding of the development officer's role is in sharp contrast with a Salesman author such as Panas, who approaches the managerial aspects of the job with little enthusiasm:

The effective fund raisers, they pulsate with joy. . . . Never bored. Excited about the work and mission. Great strategists. The drone, the drudger, the fundraiser immersed in the details and mechanics of the job will probably never raise mega gifts (1984, p. 166).

Interestingly, when Francis Pray asked a group of college and university presidents to define the role of the development officer, they often used language that suggests the Manager. Billy Wireman responded, "The two most important things development staff can do to enhance the effectiveness of the president are sound research and good organization" (Boling et al. 1981, p. 358). Richard Cheshire sees a role that contains some elements of the Catalyst, but is essentially more reactive and administrative:

The senior development officer's post is particularly tough in that it often has more responsibility than it has power and authority. Case, leadership and constituency are largely

the products of actions taken by trustees, presidents and
faculty, and yet they set the other limits of fund-raising's
reach. Where the development officer can have maximum
impact are the areas of strategy and organization (Boling
et al. 1981, p. 358).

A final example of the Manager approach is seen in the case
of Alex Carroll, a businessman and lifelong volunteer. Carroll
sees the development officer's role as largely that of the
Manager:

Although amateurs and volunteers can be counted on to
raise meaningful dollars and to help reach challenging
goals, the essential organizing both before and during any
campaign requires effective and enthusiastic inside staff
work. Asking volunteers to do the nitty gritty details is a
waste of their time and talent and abuses the privilege of
having their help (1991, p. 175).

The Leader
Some see a more significant role for the development officer
within the institution. Steven Muller, former president of Johns
Hopkins University, has written, "The staff in institutional
advancement cannot function as an adjunct to the rest of the
campus enterprise but only as an integral part of it" (1986,
p. 9). John G. Johnson advocates strong ties between the
development officer and members of the faculty: "It is essential that the development officer, as a key representative of
the university, be part of the central fabric of the institution"
(Boling et al. 1981, p. 352).

What the authors in the Leader category share is an
increased emphasis on the development officer's role as a
professional and leader within the institution. Beyond this,
however, they also emphasize a significant commitment to
development as a comprehensive enterprise—a true profession. They often refer to moral, ethical, and philosophical concerns surrounding the practice of philanthropy, and they
address expansive issues.

For example, Payton and his colleagues state, "We believe
that a professional is more than a technician. Fund-raising
practitioners without a strong ethical sense and commitment
tend to equate success with money raised—or, more precisely,
with their own income" (1991a, p. 279). Eugene Tempel sees

development as demanding "the mastery of professional technical skills that are required for fund raising and the ethical values that foster and protect philanthropy" (1991, p. 27).*

Kay Grace suggests the Leader viewpoint when she emphasizes the importance of a "professional stance [which] conveys a posture of pride rather than apology . . . [and maintains that] a professional attitude characterized by discretion, confidentiality, ethics, and integrity is vital to both the internal and external images of the development function" (1991a, p. 144). Bloland and Bornstein advocate professional advancement toward a leadership role within the institution. They write that

> *Development, the primary occupation of fund raisers, plays an increasingly central role in institutional decision making. . . . [Development] activities are organized around the core task, fund raising, but the concerns of development officers extend beyond this framework. They participate in institutional long-range and strategic planning, in relations with external individuals and organizations, and in furthering the mission of the institution* (1991, pp. 103+).

Francis Pray called for development officers to play leadership roles more than a decade ago. Summarizing the difference between a good manager of the development office and a development officer who is effective within the institution, Pray writes,

> *The poor manager, if not doomed to failure, is at least severely handicapped. But—and this is important—the good manager may not always succeed. There is another quality of the development officer, or the president or trustee, that*

---

* Professional standards should not be equated with morals or ethics in this discussion. Robert Fogal has pointed out that peer-imposed standards are not necessarily value-based. For example, the guidelines for gift accounting established by the Council for Advancement and Support of Education and the National Association of College and University Business Officers are "not intrinsic to fund raising itself." However

> *[m]any experienced fund raising executives recognize these standards and adhere to them. Persons new to the field must learn them. No practitioner considers them to be moral statements. Whether or not they are followed, however, may reflect the ethical perspectives of a fund raising professional* (1991, pp. 266-8).

is equally important: That quality is leadership. *It is the abil-ity of one person to generate enthusiasm, conviction, and action in others* (1981, p. 379).

Again, the four categories of Salesman, Catalyst, Manager, and Leader are not completely discrete, and many authors cross the boundaries separating them. But most authors clearly fall more into one category than the others, at least in terms of their bias and emphasis.

Understanding the four "schools of thought" reflected in the literature does not resolve all ambiguity regarding the development role. The fact that authors of equally impressive experience and professional recognition can hold what appear on the surface to be inconsistent views initially makes it dif-ficult to establish a consistent and integrated understanding of the development officer's role. In the next section, a para-digm will be proposed that integrates these differing view-points into a conceptual model of the development officer's role in colleges and universities today.

Summary

The history of the development function in higher education reveals the evolution of four distinct roles for the develop-ment officer. The early development officers were gift solic-itors. With the introduction of the campaign method by Ward, a role of the development officer as a catalyst was established. As development officers became full-time employees of col-leges and universities, they took on the role of manager, and as their importance grew over time, some became leaders within their institutions.

The current development literature reflects these four roles of Salesman, Catalyst, Manager, and Leader. Writers differ in their emphasis among the four roles of the development officer in a college or university. Most writers acknowledge more than one role but tend to focus on one in their writing.

Writers in the Salesman category are principally concerned with the development officer's role as a solicitor of gifts and state that the development officer should be charismatic and externally oriented. Writers of the Catalyst and Manager cate-gory state that the development officer should operate behind the scenes and generally should not be involved in soliciting gifts. Catalysts say that development officers should be direct-ing the fund-raising activities of volunteers and institutional leaders. The Managers emphasize the development officer's internal role in working with staff and providing the administrative support for fund-raising. Writers in the Leader category view the development officer as a professional and as an important figure within the institution.

Defining these four roles is the initial step toward an integrated understanding of the development officer's proper role in higher education today.

THE DEVELOPMENT OFFICER PARADIGM

Few people grow up thinking they are going to become development officers. Those now working in the field have arrived from a variety of disciplines and career paths. Most seem to have stumbled into a job and then ascended the ranks through serendipity (and hard work) as much as by strategic design. "[C]areer lines in fund raising are problematic so that it is difficult to trace a smooth upward career path" (Bloland and Bornstein 1991, p. 108).

If two university administrators with the title "comptroller" meet at a conference, their understanding of their own professional responsibilities—as well as their day-to-day tasks—probably are quite similar, even if their institutions are dissimilar. The same cannot be said of two university administrators with the title "director of development," even at similar institutions. Because there are not commonly accepted professional expectations and career paths, different assumptions exist about the role of the development officer. Some of these were discussed earlier.

This kind of disparity in job expectations and duties among practitioners results in a number of problems: It often creates difficulty for newcomers to the field in determining what responsibilities they should anticipate in their jobs; such disparity also may create a difference in expectations between development officers and their supervisors (both development staff managers and academic deans, presidents or other nondevelopment administrators); and finally, it is reflected by inconsistency among theorists and other authors in the field.

The following paradigm suggests a visual model that may help resolve these problems. The illustrations are useful in determining how various writers in the field may be categorized and more thoroughly interrelated. They also suggest a way to compare what an institution needs from its development office with what the development officer brings in experience, knowledge, and temperament. Finally, they illustrate a means to chart a career path for a particular development officer.

Internal and External Arenas

In the discussion of the development officer's role, every author recognizes that those employed in the field operate within two arenas: the internal and the external. In Figure 1, these arenas are depicted as two vectors intended to provide a model of the job responsibilities that exist within a development office.

The words "internal" and "external" refer in part to the location of the institution's constituencies within or outside of the organization. More significantly, these words also refer to the relationship between the tasks contained within the vectors and the solicitation process. Job responsibilities located on the external vector are those directly related to gift solicitation, while those on the internal vector are tasks undertaken to support these solicitations.

The vector is used as a model because it suggests a heading, a particular course to be followed. Thus, adherents to a particular school of thought may be considered to be more attuned to one vector than to the other as they progress through their careers. In addition, the vector is meant to suggest a visual representation of this career progress. The gradual broadening of the vector reflects the incremental manner in which a career often unfolds in the occupation as the development officer broadens in experience and professional interest.

The various tasks to be performed within a development office may be plotted on these vectors. Where a particular task is plotted depends upon the amount of knowledge, experience, and training required to complete the task. It will also depend upon the overall significance of that task within the institution.

On each vector, the narrow point of origin at the bottom indicates the most limited understanding and practice of the discipline, while the top represents the broadest approach to the field. For example, on the internal vector, the tasks located at the narrowest point are those associated with extreme detail, such as coding computer records or preparing gift-acknowledgment receipts. The tasks performed at this end of the internal vector are very limited in scope. Those individuals who are charged with these responsibilities are **technicians**. They are definitely necessary to the success of the entire development operation, but they usually have little direct influence over the policies of the office or institution and virtually no contact with external constituencies.

Tasks with a greater degree of responsibility are plotted at a broader part of the vector. Thus, at the mid-level the concerns are administrative in nature. A development officer who occupies a position at this level has significantly more

FIGURE 1

The Vector Paradigm

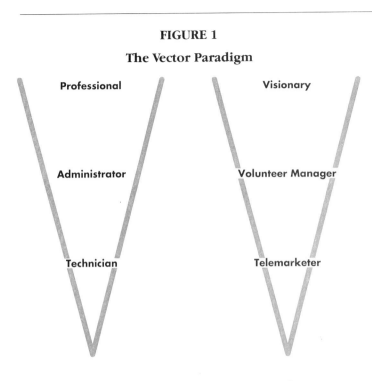

Professional

Visionary

Administrator

Volunteer Manager

Technician

Telemarketer

Internal Vector

External Vector

managerial responsibilities and therefore more influence
within the institution. As an **administrator**, the practitioners
at this point on the vector play some role in formulating policy and are charged with implementing these policies.

The top of the internal vector reflects a broad understanding
of the institution. The practitioner who occupies a position
here has an institutionwide perspective. He or she is well-
known and respected by all members of the internal constituency (deans, vice presidents, faculty, etc.). Presumably, nondevelopment colleagues within the institution consider such
an individual the "development professional" with primary
responsibility for securing philanthropic support. The professional also significantly impacts decisions affecting the institution even outside of development concerns (e.g., mission
of the institution, financing, the institutional salary and benefits package, admissions marketing, etc.). Although these are
matters of extreme importance to the institution, they are not
directly related to soliciting the gift. Thus, these tasks are
located on the internal vector.

A similar broadening of focus can be postulated on the external vector. Again, "external" here refers not only to contact with constituents outside the institution (most notably, prospective donors) but also to the tasks which are associated directly with soliciting the gift.

At the narrowest point on the external vector, the concern is with the immediate gift at hand. In the past, door-to-door solicitors were engaged at this level of fund-raising. Today, the paid telemarketer is the most common example. Jobs at the narrow end of the vector have common characteristics: The entire purpose of the contact is to solicit a gift; cultivation of the prospect is not a factor; and a deeper understanding of the prospect's motives or interests rarely is sought. The job expectations, therefore, are quite narrow and require minimal training or experience on the part of the staff member.

Further along this vector there is an increase in responsibility for solicitation programs and a concomitant increase in substantive prospect contact. At the mid-level, responsibilities are focused on management just as on the internal vector. What is different is the kind of management responsibility. On the internal vector, internal staff are managed. The external vector represents tasks associated with management of volunteers or a specific fund-raising program. So, for example, a **volunteer manager** who is responsible for organizing the 25th Reunion Gift Fund may be plotted at the mid-level of the external vector. Management of the entire Reunion Gift Program is a somewhat broader, but still mid-level, responsibility. Alternately, responsibilities represented at this level of the vector may be more specialized, such as management of the institution's Planned Giving program.

At the top of the external vector the responsibilities are the broadest. This is where the institution's vision is articulated to external constituencies. The **visionary** is the practitioner who can "paint the big picture." Typically, a development officer occupying this position deals with the very highest level of prospect and the trustees.

Overlapping Vectors

It is critical to note that these two vectors are not discrete. External solicitation responsibilities almost always are intertwined with internally based, support-oriented duties. Thus, when applied to a specific institution, the vectors will overlap to some degree. The extent and nature of the overlap depends

FIGURE 2

Overlapping Vectors

Example A
A large and mature development office

Example B
A small to mid-sized development office

Example C
A one-person development shop

upon the particular institution. Several examples are illustrated in Figure 2.

At most institutions, the vectors begin to overlap somewhere in the mid-level range. A staff member who is a middle manager probably has a degree of administrative responsibility internally and a fair amount of external contact with volunteers and others. At the narrowest end of the vector, job responsibilities do not overlap; the person who programs the computer probably is not responsible for making phonathon solicitations, except in the very smallest development shops.

A development officer who occupies a position at the broadest point of these vectors experiences a great deal of overlap. To fulfill these very broad responsibilities, the development officer must possess an understanding of the institution as well as the ability to effectively communicate this understanding to motivate the highest-level donor.

Generally, the larger the development operation, the further up the vector the overlap begins. Figure 2, Example A illustrates a large and mature development operation. With scores of staff members, for example, only a few individuals have positions that could be plotted at the broadest part of the vectors. Only a few most senior staff members have both external and internal responsibilities that overlap. On the other hand, the great majority of individuals employed in a large development office are more narrowly focused, specializing in a particular area or program with little or no overlap between vectors.

Figure 2, Example B illustrates a smaller development office. In these small development operations, the vectors may overlap to a great degree; this is commonly referred to as "wearing many hats." Fewer staff members are employed, meaning that fewer are highly specialized. This also means that fewer jobs may be plotted exclusively within either the internal or external vectors.

Finally, Figure 2, Example C demonstrates the complete overlap within a one-person development shop. Since one staff member is responsible for all development activities, all job duties—from the narrowest to the broadest—are the purview of that single individual.

Visualizing development office tasks using this paradigm assists the development theorist and practitioner in three ways: 1) It assists in the analysis and classification of the literature in the field; 2) it illustrates what a specific institution needs from its development office in terms of organization and the responsibilities of the staff; and 3) it helps pinpoint a particular development officer's own position with the organization relative to these institutional circumstances and thereby assists in planning a possible career path.

Integrating the Literature

The vector model provides a way to review and analyze the literature. As discussed in section two, there are four general approaches to understanding the role of the development officer. The literature of each of these schools of thought focuses on only a part of this whole illustration. Each author, while aware of the totality, limits (intentionally or unintentionally) the discussion to a particular range depending upon the purpose of the piece, personal interests and underlying assumptions about development. These specific ways of thinking about the role may be plotted on the vector paradigm, as shown in Figure 3.

FIGURE 3

Integrating the Literature with the Vector Paradigm

Example A
Salesman Approach

Example B
Catalyst Approach

Example C
Manager Approach

Example D
Leader Approach

Authors who write from the Salesman perspective focus almost exclusively on the concerns represented by the external vector. Practitioners who adopt the Salesman approach demonstrate little patience for internal administrative matters but a great deal of interest in directly soliciting gifts. Salesman authors tend to focus on one of two areas within the external vector, as illustrated by Figure 3, Example A. Those whose concerns are narrower describe job responsibilities closely aligned with those of the telemarketer. "How to" books are an example, detailing, as they do, specific ways to make an approach, to deal with those who refuse to consider a gift, to negotiate a larger gift from prospects who are wavering, and so forth.

Other Salesman authors take a broader perspective. They deal in larger and grander schemes. Many use the vocabulary of the visionary, and their area of concern may be delineated on a broader part of the vector. However, Salesmen authors tend not to concern themselves with internal issues of professional institutional leadership. Therefore, the areas they address are appropriately limited to the external vector.

Authors of the Catalyst tradition also deal primarily with matters on the external vector (Figure 3, Example B). Catalysts tend to be "sandwiched" between the interest areas of the Salesmen. The Catalyst's areas of interest coincide with the job duties of the volunteer manager. This makes sense, because Catalysts focus on the external tasks of gift solicitation. They do not anticipate making the solicitations themselves, but rather to cause others to solicit on the institution's behalf. Catalysts may become involved with internal matters to a degree, because they do have to undertake some administrative tasks to staff volunteer committees. Therefore, their concerns include some area of overlap into the internal vector.

By contrast, authors in the Manager category attend almost exclusively to matters on the internal vector (Figure 3, Example C). However, Managers have a relatively deep range of concern within the internal vector. Therefore, authors and practitioners with a Manager's mind-set deal with both narrow internal concerns, such as data record maintenance, and broader administrative issues of policy and complex procedures. Because they do not overlap with issues on the external vector, however, Managers rarely concern themselves with the broadest areas of institutional concern represented by the very top of the vectors.

The broadest approach is pursued by authors and practitioners in the Leader category, as shown in Figure 3, Example D. By definition, those who write or practice from this perspective are interested in the broadest approach possible. They are concerned with being recognized as professionals within the organization—indeed, they are at the forefront of the move toward recognizing development as a profession, to be discussed below. Leaders view this orientation as essential to fulfill the vision they present to prospective major donors. In fact, Leaders believe that a firm grounding in professionalism, as practiced within the institution, is necessary to prevent a visionary appeal from becoming illusory rhetoric.

Institutional Needs

The vector paradigm also provides a way to think about what a particular institution needs from its development operation. If resources will not allow the hiring of many staff, the positions that can be funded must be carefully selected. By determining the degree of overlap that is realistic for the specific institution, it is also possible to get a sense for the ratio of employees who can specialize in exclusively internal or exclusively external positions, in relation to the number of generalists needed.

For example, if a small institution's development office profile is similar to that shown in Figure 2, Example B, there will be little room for specialization. Therefore, if a disproportionate percentage of staff resources are committed to the internal vector, the number and quality of personal cultivation and solicitation visits are probably suffering as a result, and the institution will not achieve its philanthropic potential. On the other hand, if too many staff resources are committed externally relative to internal support staff, there will be a lack of solid and reliable underpinnings to the development program. Thus, long-term philanthropic growth may be jeopardized.

These assessments are quite subjective, and the individual making the determination of how much is too much is also influenced by his or her own view of what role the development officer should play. However, this model provides a basis for discussion among those responsible for the development office's success.

If too many staff resources are committed externally relative to internal support staff, there will be a lack of solid and reliable underpinnings to the development program.

The Development Career

Finally, the vector paradigm may be used to guide an individual in thinking about his or her own career position and path. There are several ways this model may be so used. Figure 4 illustrates a development office in which specific job roles are plotted.

FIGURE 4

The Vector Paradigm and Specific Job Descriptions

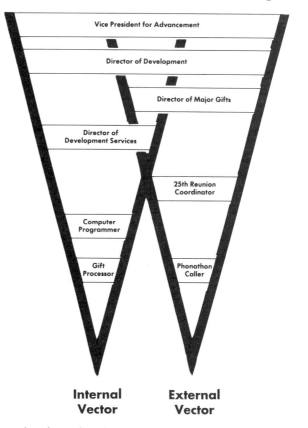

As stated, tasks within the development office include some
with internal characteristics, some with external characteristics,
and some that overlap. Each position within the office can
be plotted on the vector paradigm. Examples are provided
in Figure 4. In almost every office (the one-person shop being
the exception), there are jobs available at the very narrowest
end of the vectors that may be characterized as either exclusively internal or exclusively external. More senior positions
may be plotted at various places on the vectors. Some of these
positions will be primarily internal (e.g., director of development services). Others may be largely external (e.g., director of major gifts). All of these positions will exhibit some
degree of overlap, however. Finally, at the very broadest levels, the chief development officer should occupy a position

of significant overlap between the vectors.

For an individual contemplating entry into the development field, it would be helpful to decide to which vector his or her skills and interests are best suited. This provides practical guidance as to what types of positions one might pursue. The ongoing maturation of development as an occupational option has meant that a wider variety of careers are feasible. It is possible to have an important and fulfilling career while filling a position on either vector. This model suggests ways a career path might be planned. And while it is by no means uncommon for people in the development field to jump from one type of position to another, there is increasingly the ability to grow within the occupation by broadening areas of responsibility and experience in a more systematic fashion, beginning on either vector.

The vector paradigm may also be helpful in identifying appropriate "fits" (or "misfits") between a particular development officer and a specific institution. For example, after careful consideration, the development officer may decide that his or her own style and predilection would point to a career as a Salesman. If, after further reflection, he or she determines that an institution has a need and a desire for aggressive people spending virtually all of their time working directly with donors—and the development staff is large enough so that basic systems can be maintained internally by others—that individual may decide that he or she would fit well within the organization. On the other hand, if the institution already has many people directly soliciting gifts but needs more people to administer its internal resources, then a staff member with a strong Manager orientation would be a better choice. If the institution has a strong and vibrant volunteer tradition that is cherished, then a Catalyst may best be able to fulfill the organization's needs.

Summary
The tasks to be achieved within a development office—and the responsibilities staff members assume to achieve these tasks—may be illustrated by using the vector paradigm. This model suggests that development functions operate in two arenas: internal and external. External tasks are those directly related to soliciting gifts. Internal tasks are undertaken to support the solicitation process.

On the internal vector, these support tasks range from the

very narrow to the broad. At the narrowest point, the development staff member is a technician and is responsible for specific, well-defined achievements, such as maintaining address lists. At the mid-level on the internal vector, development officers are administrators, and their responsibilities are broader, including policy matters and implementation of procedures. At the broadest level of this vector, the development officer functions as a professional and is responsible for integrating a profound knowledge of the institution's mission and strategic plan with the overall fund-raising program.

A similar broadening of responsibilities is reflected on the external vector related to direct solicitations. At the narrowest point, the responsibilities are those of a telemarketer, whose only responsibility is to ask for a gift. At the mid-level, the development officer is a volunteer manager whose responsibilities revolve around staffing volunteers and externally focused programs. At the broadest level on the external vector, the visionary deals with trustees, major donors, and others who make a significant difference to the institution. Solicitation at this level involves considerable cultivation and knowledge of the prospect's interests. The development officer invests a great deal of time informing the prospect about the institution and its aspirations before the actual solicitation takes place.

When applied to a specific institution, the two vectors overlap to a greater or lesser degree. Large development operations have little overlap, indicating the presence of more narrowly focused, highly specialized jobs. Small development shops have greater overlap. Development staff in these offices tend to have both internal and external responsibilities; they "wear many hats."

The vector paradigm may be used in three ways: 1) to categorize authors in the field according to their school of thought; 2) to analyze what an institution needs from its development officers; and 3) to suggest ways an individual may plan a career within the development field, particularly as it relates to personal interests and aptitudes.

PHILOSOPHICAL QUESTIONS

The development literature includes discussion of a number of philosophical questions. The viewpoints of various authors on these issues reveal their positions in the Salesman, Catalyst, Manager, or Leader categories. There are also a number of practical issues related to who should be involved in the fundraising process and how it should be conducted. Authors' opinions about the practical questions are often a reflection of their positions about the philosophical questions, four of which are discussed in this section.

1. What personality traits are required for success as a development officer?
2. Is development an art or a science, innate or learnable?
3. What is the appropriate motivation for entry into a career in development?
4. Is development a "profession"?

What Personality Traits Are Required of the Successful Development Officer?

There are a number of points of agreement among all authors regarding the desirable personality traits of the development officer. Generally, everyone believes the development officer should be well-rounded, intelligent, personable, capable, and gifted in communication. In short, he or she should be all things to all people. As Charles McCord puts it, "People in our business have got to be in the 'Renaissance Man' mold" (1981, p. 371). Panas is somewhat more baroque in his answer to this question:

> One thing is certain, fundraisers are a totally dissimilar group. They look different. Act differently. Work differently. They are diverse—hard charging and hard driving, quietly effective. They include used-car salesmen types, ministers and priests, scholars and backslappers. Computer freaks and computer-frightened. Great writers and virtually illiterate. They do not have the same characteristics or personalities (1988, p. 8).

Despite these broad laundry-list descriptions, however, the answer to this question depends in large part upon the author's position in the Salesman, Catalyst, Manager, or Leader school. If one assumes the development officer should be on the road soliciting major gifts, different personality traits will be sought than if one assumes the development officer keeps the books balanced and the shop running. The issue is to determine the appropriate mix of development officer as a low-key, desk-bound administrator and as an active external voice sharing the institutional vision in a charismatic fashion.

The Salesmen are consistent, advocating an emphasis on the latter. Panas grants that it is often necessary to work on technical matters behind the scenes, but this is not where he believes the real work of the development officer lies:

> *Technical skills are primarily concerned with working with 'things.' Writing copy for a folder, developing a proposal for a grant, understanding direct response mail, purchasing precisely the right software for your computer. These are important, but usually at a lower level in the development office. . . . The soul and spirit of fundraising is a beguiling blend of needs and desires, grind and gratifications. The alchemy of sacrifice and personal contribution goes far beyond any material reward we could hope for. This business, it is the ultimate venture. Those who are inspired and successful in the field live each day as the wildest of all explorations. The chance to catch a close view of things seen never before* (1988, pp. 94+).

Those in the Leader category tend to agree with the Salesmen on this point. Payton points out the necessity of interpersonal skills: "If you really like books or numbers better than people, you are not likely to enjoy development work or do it well" (1981, p. 284). In Frick's experience, "The most effective advancement people I know have an absolute zest for fundraising. To this individual the prospective benefactor is like a battle to be won, a stream to be forded, a mountain to be climbed" (1986, p. 364). Pray agrees, writing,

> *If a development officer . . . cannot occasionally hear at least an echo of the great 'poem' that is, ideally, the process of opening up human potential through education, and does not have the ability to transmit some of the awe and inspiration of that poem to those who can help make it a reality, that person should step aside for one who can* (1981, p. 381).

While the Catalysts and the Managers do not disparage this ability to community effectively, they do relegate this aspect of the development officer role to a subordinate position. Or perhaps Catalysts and Managers just communicate more softly: "The wise staff will never need to have imposed upon it the policy that its role is quiet and effective service rather than overt leadership" (Seymour 1966, p. 117). J. Patrick Ryan believes, "It is not a high visibility thing that we do, and if we become high visibility, we have probably lost some of our effectiveness" (Harrah-Conforth and Borsos 1991, p. 29).

Berendt and Taft sound a similar theme; among the traits of a good development officer, they include being "a good pest . . . secure, aggressive, and persistent enough to 'bug' your trustees and other volunteers consistently without fear of rejection" (1983, p. 35). This implies a certain subservient role to the volunteers. As Richard Colton, retired director of development at Dartmouth College, notes dryly, "Be sure your ego is in good shape because you will need to have a passion for anonymity" ("Capsules of Advice" 1981, p. 375). This is in sharp contrast to the view of a Salesman such as Panas, who asserts that "the great fundraisers all have presence. . . . These men and women, they fill a room" (1988, p. 48).

In terms of personal style, proponents of all points of view seem to agree that the development officer must not stand out too much and must not be seen as too unconventional or too controversial. Seymour's advice is often echoed in the literature:

Proponents of all points of view seem to agree that the development officer must not stand out too much.

> *It may seem needlessly elementary, but it is worth reminding recruits about xenophobia—fear of the stranger. Too much difference from expected or normal standards, in matters of dress, comportment, habits of speech, knife and fork drill, and so on, will at the least be distracting, and at the worst can upset confidence* (1966, p. 182).

Berendt and Taft advocate that development officers be non-controversial in terms which might give pause to the institution's Equal Opportunity Employment officer. They advise chief executive officers to

> *Consider—unfair though it may be—the appearance, dress, and general social background of the person you are choosing. Development directors must be able to create an almost*

peer relationship with board members and staff. If board members are largely an "Ivy League" conservative bunch, it doesn't make much sense to hire someone who will conflict basically with their images and value systems. Enough said (1983, pp. 35-36).

Is Development an Art or a Science, Innate or Learnable?

This question has yielded the most muddled answers in the literature. Often, the author wants to have it both ways. Panas, for example, considers this issue at length, and then summarizes:

Innate or learnable? Achievable by anyone? This is the overriding question which gives substance and soul to my work and research. I think that the proof is conclusive. . . . Fundraising is less a science of mechanics and organizational structure than it is the art of persuasion and motivation. Some concentrate on the 'how' of fundraising, but that's the science. The real winners focus of the 'why' and that is the art of this business. . . . It's a continuing debate, with no definitive answers. . . . Learned or taught, it is quite clear that the great fundraisers are not 'made' overnight. Nor are they simply 'born.' It is almost certainly a happy combination of the two (1988, pp. 169-71).

Again, however, there is a tendency for the Salesmen and those adhering to the Leader category to see this issue differently from the Catalysts and Managers. The former refer again and again to the art of fund-raising; the ability to do so effectively is either innate or learned at an early age. To quote Panas again, "The great fundraisers know all of the principles, basics, and the mechanics. They know their trade and apply it well. But most of all, they follow their intuition" (1988, p. 12). He goes on to give an example:

[I]f a museum, for instance, is looking for a really effective fundraiser, it is almost certain that the least important criterion is to seek a person who has museum experience. Trust me. I am right on this. Look instead for someone with the right mix of qualities. The language of the institution or the discipline can be learned easily. The magic of fundraising cannot (1988, p. 112).

On the other hand, Catalysts and Managers emphasize the techniques and established practices of fund-raising. These can be taught and learned, of course—presumably by anyone of reasonable intelligence. Murray, who reflects a Manager orientation, believes that the art vs. science debate is "an unnecessary division." To Murray,

> As in all professions (medicine, law, teaching), fund raising is an art. It is the skillful application of technical and inter-personal know-how to the circumstances found in given situations. The art or practice of fund raising will become a more mature profession as we develop an underlying body of knowledge to support it. As this body of knowledge becomes clear, pertinent, and well organized, it comprises a science. Fund raisers will then be able to draw principles, concepts and techniques from this body of knowledge to help them in their work (1987, p. 5).

Catalysts, such as Brakeley, tend to believe that "successful fund raising depends on the steady application of various techniques" (1980, p. ix) rather than esoteric "artful" knowl-edge. Frantzreb attempts to illustrate these techniques with step-by-step instructions:

> The manner of seeking the appointment, personal dress, eye-to-eye contact, smile, thanks to a secretary, compliments on the office or home or club—each and all constitute the "first impression" even if the solicitor and prospect have met before. . . . Compliment the prospect appropriately, fre-quently, but not to the point of distraction. Draw out busi-ness, family, professional, and civic interests for temporary mental diversion. Then reintroduce the mission, the role, and the importance of the prospect and the organization's grateful appreciation (1991, pp. 123+).

David Ketchum, one of the early generation of Catalysts, writes,

> Despite the ever-increasing nuances in the profession, how-ever, there are still fundamental principles and disciplines required for success. During the next ten years, I think most of the soft-headed theorizing and high-level mystery now encountered will have been soundly disproved and there

will be greater adherence to the axioms on which successful fund raising has been, is, and will be based ("Capsules of Advice" 1981, pp. 372-3).

In contrast with Panas, Broce maintains, "There is no magic in fundraising. The skills are primarily those of effective planning, organization, management, and marketing, bolstered by good common sense" (1979, p. 5).

Seymour is characteristically straightforward on this question: "Only fools and fatheads, in my experience, ever seek to build an image of the special cult, the mystique, and the ways of an inscrutable expertise" (1966, p. 118).

What Is the Appropriate Motivation for Entering a Development Career?

The answers given to this question tend to revolve around two poles: development as a calling or development as a career. Authors of all persuasions can be found circling either pole, perhaps depending upon their own level of comfort in using religious or spiritual metaphors.

It has been suggested that there is a natural tension between these views that has existed throughout the historical evolution of the field (Harrah-Conforth and Borsos 1991, pp. 19, 27). The earliest fund-raisers (the college presidents) usually were ministers. This service orientation—service to God and to mankind—has been passed along, to some extent, even to the present day, as evidenced by the use of terms such as "value-based" and "mission" to describe the fund-raising process (Rosso 1991, p. 4; Tempel 1991, p. 23).

Expressions of the "missionary" nature of this job cut across lines. A Salesman such as Panas clearly believes in fund-raising as a calling:

> *The great fundraisers always seem to pass the same litmus test: Their profession is not merely a higher calling, it is missionary work. . . . [I]f you are not in this business because you have a strong tug of religious and spiritual consciousness, your fundraising work will not be operating on full cylinders* (1988, pp. 34, 52).

However, a Catalyst such as Brakeley also uses inspirational language: "Idealism—the belief in a particular cause or causes which are part of a larger cause and a larger purpose—is a primary motivation for the majority of men and women attracted to and working in the fund-raising profession today" (1980, p. 7). Rosso refers to giving as a privilege and his own

> *belief that people draw a creative energy, a sense of self-worth, a capacity to function productively from sources beyond themselves. This is a deep personal belief or a religious conviction. . . . The solicitation should be so executed as to demonstrate to the prospective contributor that there can be a joy to giving* (1991, p. 6).

Broce, who has characteristics of both Manager and Catalyst, also uses religious terminology:

> *Most people enter the fund-raising profession not because it is an easy way to make a living but because it is a tangible way in which they can marshal their talents to serve others. The excitement that comes with raising money [lies] . . . in that glow one feels when the person with the skills to make things happen comes in contact with a person with the resources to make an investment that will pay significant benefits to many generations. When these two come together, they move mountains* (1979, p. 3).

Some advocates of active institutional leadership echo this language. Frick, for example, says the development role

> *is a noble one in my judgment. It is worthy of dedicated men and women. It can, and should, be a vocation, even in a kind of religious sense. Not everyone is called to such work* (1986, p. 370).

However, among others in the Leader category, this religious terminology is replaced with an orientation toward a philosophical language emphasizing theory and research. Rejecting both religious and business metaphors, they strive to define the field in terms of the academy.

Payton and his colleagues at the Indiana University Center on Philanthropy, for example, recommend that fund-raising be studied within the context of the liberal arts.

*The liberal arts lack an answer to the fund-raising ques-
tions: Why do you exist? Why should anyone give you
money? We believe that the liberal arts would be stronger
and more influential both within the university and outside
it if philosophers, historians, and sociologists were more
immediately engaged in fund raising, more attentive to their
mission and their case* (1991a, p. 278).

Schrum also suggests a broader educational role:

*After all, we call ourselves educational fund raisers. That
can simply mean that we raise money for education. But
it can also mean that we have an educational role to play
as well as a fund-raising role* (1993, p. 365).

Bloland and Bornstein maintain that it is essential that fund-
raisers commit themselves to a professional approach. They
propose thinking of this issue as a matrix, with high or low
orientation to the occupation on one axis, and high or low
orientation to the institution on the other. Clearly, they advocate high commitment to both occupation and institution,
although they recognize the difficulty in maintaining both
(1991, pp. 106-7).

FIGURE 5

Professional Approach to Development*

		Orientation to Occupation (Cosmopolitanism)	
		+	−
Orientation to Institution (Localism)	+	Professional	Booster
	−	Careerist (Migrant Worker)	Placebound Worker

---

*From Bloland and Bornstein (1991), p. 106.

It is widely recognized that fund-raising is "the job of trained professionals working with dedicated volunteers who also have some expertise in the art" (Broce 1979, p. 4). Those in the Leader category who call for increased professionalism view this as a problem: "Sharing expertise with amateurs considerably weakens the occupation's power to define its work and establish jurisdictional control and legitimacy" (Bloland and Bornstein 1991, p. 105). Their proposed solution to this problem is the development of a theory base within the academy:

> *The generation of basic theory adds greatly to occupational control. Although the work of fund raising by full-time people is shared with amateurs, if a theory and research base is in the hands of professionals, the distinctions between professional and amateur can be more sharply drawn, and fund raising can have a greater ability to define and defend its work boundaries (1991, p. 117).*

These authors see development work as very important, but not in terms of a calling from God. Rather, it is seen as centered on man and on individual action and therefore is an appropriate study of the humanities.* As Payton and colleagues put forth in a sort of manifesto:

> *Thinking of fund raising as a First Amendment right is a reminder that fund raising is an exercise in voluntary association and free speech. If there is merit in that view, fund*

---

* As an aside, it is interesting to note that in the past some have tried to define the development process in more objective ways, although their efforts have not been research based. Frantzreb, for example, outlined the following "diagrammatic formula" for understanding the development function (1970, p. 16):

$$\frac{A\,(B/S) + P\,(A/F) + N/O}{C + C^2 + P(R) + V} \quad x\ DP \quad \left(\frac{(\ \ B + S\ \ )}{(A + C + D)}\right) \quad (S/G) = \$\$$$

A = authenticators	C = case	DP = development plan
B = governing board	C² = conditioning	B = Budget
S = sponsors/council	P = prospects	S = staff
P = plans	R = research	A = annual
A = academic	V = volunteers	C = capital
F = financial		D = deferred giving
N = needs		S = schedule
O = opportunities		G = goals

raising is ennobled by it. Bringing fund raising into the uni-
versity is simple recognition of the importance of fund rais-
ing as a form of voluntary action. Our hope is that fund
raising will be taken seriously (1991a, pp. 280-1).

However, this too is a kind of calling: Fund-raising is not just
a job, but a very "serious," self-aware (and perhaps self-
conscious) undertaking.

Is Development a "Profession"?

The terms "profession" and "professional" have been used
throughout this volume to refer to the development function
and development officers. This terminology is often used in
the literature by authors of all four categories, but as discussed
above, the view of the development officer as a true "professional" is one particularly emphasized by writers of the Leader
school.

However, the term profession is often used in a casual way
that diminishes its meaning:

> *The words "profession" or professional" creep into the ever-*
> *yday language of just about everyone. As is often the case,*
> *overuse of a word correlates highly with the loss of its real*
> *meaning. . . .*
>
> *What people are talking about and writing about, of course,*
> *are vocations or occupations. Everyone knows what these*
> *words mean, but using them to modify the proper name*
> *of the work somebody does in awkward. Who would want*
> *to say, "I'm an occupational house painter," or "There goes*
> *a vocational barber?" Besides, using the term "professional"*
> *adds a note of class to the occupation, because we all know*
> *that professions enjoy prestige, approbation, and public*
> *recognition* (Carbone 1989, p. 9).

There is a consensus among writers on the subject that development has not yet become a true profession in the sense
of medicine or law. However, there are shades of difference
in their conclusions on the question.

In a 1989 study, Carbone defines six characteristics of a profession: autonomy of decision making, a systematic body of
knowledge and skills, self-regulation and collegial standard

setting, commitment to and identification with the profession, altruism and dedication to service, and a code of ethics with accompanying sanctions (1989, p. 27). He provides his own analysis of development on the basis of these criteria and reports the findings of a survey of development officers' views.

He concludes that development is an "emerging profession":

Despite what some highly regarded fund raising practition-ers assert, it must be concluded that fund raising is not yet a profession. At least, it is not among those few occupations that society generally recognizes as true professions, albeit true professions with warts and faults and problems. Evi-dence exists, however, supporting the conclusion that fund raising is an emerging profession—an occupation that has moved steadily along the professional continuum; an occu-pation with the potential to attain greater professional stat-ure (1989, p. 46).

However, Carbone doubts that development will ever achieve status as a "true" profession like medicine or law:

In all candor, true professional status for fund raisers may be an "unreachable star," but greater professional stature is certainly possible. By reaching for that star, fund raisers can accelerate progress along the continuum and thus hasten fund raising's professional maturity (1989, p. 46).

Like most authors on the subject, Carbone is writing broadly about development officers in all types of nonprofit organi-zations. Only 41 percent of the practicing development offi-cers included in his 1989 survey were working in colleges and universities (1989, p. 23). Focusing on higher education, Peter Buchanan, president of the Council for Advancement and Support of Education, agrees that fund-raising or devel-opment will never be recognized as a true profession. But, he holds greater hope for the broader field of institutional advancement:

I do not believe that fund raising, or educational fund rais-ing, in its narrowest conception will ever be considered seriously as a profession. On the other hand, advancement in its broadest conception is already considered a profession by a precious few, whose numbers will grow rapidly as that broader conception is better defined and more wisely communicated to the public (1993, p. 368).

Citing "most critics and scholars," Buchanan identifies three characteristics of a profession: "a high level of expertise in a well-grounded field of knowledge, the development of a strong theoretical base for that field, and ongoing research in the field" (1993, p. 370). Citing Carbone, he adds five others: "a full-time activity, a code of ethics, a professional association, professional training in higher education, and certification of expertise" (1993, p. 371).

To establish advancement as a profession, Buchanan calls for agreement on the definitions of "institutional advancement," "fund-raising" and "marketing"; greater integration of the various institutional advancement functions and their professional organizations; more research to formulate a theoretical basis for the field; professional graduate education programs; recognition and endorsement of the institutional advancement field by educational leaders; and a greater commitment to service on the part of practitioners. His discussion returns to the question discussed earlier in this report about the proper motivation for entering the development field:

[I] would submit that at the heart of educational advancement must be an unshakable belief that its effective practice is a moral commitment in service to education, and hence to society. Only with such a central belief can advancement be a full-fledged family member in its own house and have its practice fully accepted as a profession by the public (1993, p. 378).

Most writers see development's movement toward greater professionalism and professional status as desirable for the individuals and the higher education institutions they serve. Buchanan cites a "bipolar" answer to the question of why professionalism is desirable, saying that "on the one hand, the determination of professionalism is self-serving . . . [but that] [m]oving toward the professional end of the spectrum has significant benefits [for institutions] as well as some admitted self-serving characteristics" (1993, p. 369).

Buchanan cites situations in which an advancement officer does not have sufficient authority within his or her institution, saying such circumstances are detrimental to the institution and the individual because they "[p]revent a practitioner from working effectively and, hence, of being fairly evaluated and held accountable for results" (1993, p. 369).

For the individual, professional status brings respect, admiration, trust, and high incomes. Buchanan asks, "Who among us would not wish to be so described?" (1993, p. 371).

However, Worth sounds a cautionary note regarding the professionalization of college and university development officers, writing:

> *We have come to view professionalism in fund raising as a good thing. And, surely if by that we mean adherence to high standards of ethics and performance, it is. But we have seen in other fields that an increased professional consciousness also can be to the detriment of institutions. It has happened with faculty in many fields, who gain their identity and recognition more through their association with colleagues in the same discipline nationwide than within their individual institutions. This focus on professional field rather than institution, combined with high mobility, has been widely observed as diminishing institutional loyalty and faculty participation in institutional concerns. If this tendency is troubling with regard to professors, it is potentially disastrous with regard to development officers, whose responsibility and sole purpose is the advancement of the college or university (1993, p. 406).*

Stephen Joel Trachtenberg, president of George Washington University, also sounds warnings, urging development officers not to become "professionally arrogant" (1993, p. 21). Elaborating on this concern, he writes:

> *What I mean is the kind of "doctor knows best" attitude of which some people have accused the medical profession— the attitude that what we do is a science and unfathomable to mere laypeople. Folks resent that in doctors, and they resent it in development officers (1993, p. 21).*

Summary

The literature includes a debate on various philosophical questions. The positions that individual writers take regarding these questions reflect their positions in the Salesman, Catalyst, Manager, or Leader category.

With regard to the personality traits required for success as a development officer, writers in the Salesman and Leader categories tend to emphasize interpersonal and communication skills. Writers in the Catalyst and Manager categories tend to minimize the importance of such skills and focus on the development officer's need to stay behind the scenes.

Many writers do not give a clear answer to the question of whether development is an art or a science and whether the skills it requires are innate or learnable. However, writers in the Salesman and Leader categories tend to discuss development as an "art," requiring some innate personality traits, while Catalysts and Managers are more concerned with technical skills that can be learned.

Writers are divided on whether development is a "calling" or a "career"—that is, on whether development officers should be people principally motivated by commitment to the institution or by personal rewards. Some writers discuss fund-raising in the context of "philanthropy" and emphasize ethical and spiritual issues.

On the question of whether development is a true "profession" in the sense of medicine and law, there is a consensus that it continues to move in the direction of a profession but that it can only be considered an "emerging profession" at best and likely will never achieve full recognition of professional status. A few writers express concern that an increasing professional identity may lead development officers away from commitment to their institutions and toward the "professional arrogance" of which other professions are sometimes accused.

PRACTICAL QUESTIONS

Among the practical questions addressed in the literature, four appear most central to the work of the practitioner development officer in higher education:
1. What should be the development officer's relationship to the president?
2. What should be the development officer's relationship to the trustees?
3. What should be the development officer's role in institutional planning?
4. Who should solicit the gift?

The answers to these questions, of course, depend upon the perspective of the author. Writers of the Salesman approach see the development officer as an independent operator, reliant on his or her own initiative and one-to-one interaction with the donor. They emphasize the development officer's involvement in soliciting gifts and tend to neglect the importance of the president or the trustees in the development process.

Writers of the catalyst viewpoint see the development officer as a key player on a "fund-raising team" that includes the president and the board of trustees. In this view, fund-raising will only be successful if all three parties "desire a relationship, understand their specific roles, work diligently within their roles, have agreed upon goals, and [are] mutually supportive" (Kinnison and Ferin 1989, p. 58). Writers of the Leader category emphasize the role of the development officer as an institutional officer, with implications for the role that he or she should play in setting institutional priorities.

What Should Be the Development Officer's Relationship to the President?

Most writers emphasize the importance of the president's leadership in fund-raising success and view the development officer in a Catalyst or Manager role. Indeed, most presidents who have written or spoken on the subject focus on the development officer as Catalyst or Manager.

George N. Rainsford, former president of Kalamazoo College, states that "the president, if he is really doing his fund-raising job, is the chief development officer of the college. The development officers work for him; he does not work for them. . . ." The development officer should "maintain a flow of good information and research about key prospects"

Indeed, most presidents who have written or spoken on the subject focus on the development officer as Catalyst or Manager.

(Boling et al. 1981, pp. 353-4).

Rainsford, in particular, sees a limited role for the development officer:

> *the president has to sell the whole institution rather than just the single purpose that is the object of the solicitation call. The development officer has to understand that the case of the institution must be greater than the case for any single need. The president is the one best able to sell the entire institution. . . . [F]und raising has to be part of institutional planning, but institutional planning must precede serious fund raising. The development officer is not the chief actor in this planning. The president and the academic officer are* (Boling et al. 1981, pp. 353-4).

R. Miller Upton, former president of Beloit College, is equally clear on this point. In his view, the development officer's

> *most important responsibility is that of helping the president and, through the president, helping members of the board of trustees to raise the major funds, the capital gifts. This is why, you see, I react so adversely to the criticism by a president that the development director isn't getting out and raising money. He can't and he shouldn't. He's wasting his time. He should be building organization for you* (1970, p. 30).

Dennis Murray, who rose through the ranks as a development officer to become president of Marist College, shares this view to a large degree, writing that

> *the most successful development officers in America are managers of fund-raising activities and not merely fund raisers. True, many accomplished development officers are very effective at securing gifts, but, more importantly, they direct the overall process that results in successful gift solicitation* (1987, p. 5).

Like the presidents, William McGoldrick, a development officer, places the major responsibility on the president, whom he sees as "both the principal author of the vision and, as the university's chief advocate, the ultimate asker for big money" (1993, p. 154). McGoldrick's view of the chief development officer's goal is managerial: "The vice president is responsible for preparing the campaign strategy, executing campaign plans, and organizing the time and activities the president and trustees devote to the campaign" (1993, p. 154).

Fisher, a former university president and former president of the Council for Advancement and Support of Education, is unusual among presidents in addressing the development officer's role in the terminology of the Leader authors. Addressing himself to new college presidents, Fisher advises:

> *Advancement professionals are first and foremost educators . . . you must sincerely include your fund-raising vice president in all substantive discussions about the institution and its affairs. . . . Advancement officers aren't tradespersons; they are professionals. And in higher education, the only sure way they can be truly committed to the mission is to be considered full-fledged members of the team* (1989, p. 10).

Characteristically iconoclastic, Kelly maintains that "[m]uch of the fund-raising literature incorrectly refers to presidents as the chief fund raisers for their institutions [and that] such an assumption contributes to the myth of the invisible fund raiser . . ." (1991, p. 153).

A number of writers emphasize the relationship between the president and chief development officer as essential to fund-raising success. "[T]he president's relationship with professional development staff, and particularly the chief development officer, is pivotal" (Patton 1993, p. 54). And a number of authors provide advice on developing and maintaining this relationship.

Fisher encourages new presidents to select their vice president for development on two criteria: "track record and chemistry." He explains:

> *I have known presidents who feel so foreign in the company of fund-raising activities and people that they appoint to their top position a person with an impressive resume but who makes them feel uncomfortable. Almost invariably they later regret their choice and engage in the even more uncomfortable task of getting rid of the person* (1989, p. 8).

Consistent with his emphasis on personal chemistry, Fisher diminishes the importance of having a "professional" as chief development officer. He urges presidents to "go with chemistry over experience" if they cannot find a qualified person for the chief development officer position (1989, pp. 8-9).

Trachtenberg agrees with Fisher on the importance of chemistry, but adds a second requirement:

> *I think there are two basic requirements for a successful working partnership between a president and a development officer. The first is intangible—personal chemistry. The second is a* common understanding of roles (1991, emphasis added).

Trachtenberg explicitly recognizes the multiple development roles and the difficulty in defining the development officer's job, asking:

> *Is he or she principally an officer of the institution with a broad institutional responsibility, or just a hired gun who raises money for whatever schemes presidents and their faculties may come up with? Is he or she a salesman, or a sales manager? Is he or she principally a staff officer, or a line manager? If all of these, then in what proportion?* (1991)

And, Trachtenberg believes that a lack of common understanding of roles is a problem in the relationship between presidents and their development officers:

> *I am not convinced that in all situations the president and the chief development officer view their jobs the same way and have a common understanding of each other's role. Obviously, in a great many cases presidents and their development officers have worked these things out and their relationships are going along just fine. But the high turnover among development officers, some of it involuntary, and the frustrations I hear some presidents and development officers express about each other suggest to me that not all of them are playing the game by the same rule book* (1991).

What Should Be the Development Officer's Relationship to Trustees?

Those who view development as a process involving a "three-party relationship" place considerable emphasis on the importance of the board of trustees. Pocock is adamant: "No matter for what purpose—operational or personal—the trustee must be a key participant if the fund-raising program is to succeed" (1989, p. 4).

> *The simple answer to the question "Why trustees?" is that the board is the ultimate seat of power and responsibility in the institution. Among the many charges to the board is that of ensuring adequate resources are and will be available to support the programs of the institution* (1989, p. 3).

And, the involvement of the trustees must go beyond policy and planning to an active role in fund-raising. The maxim that trustees should "give, get, or get off" (Kinnison and Ferin 1989, p. 57) is commonly mentioned in the literature. Stuhr extends the trustees' involvement to a participatory role in all aspects of the fund-raising process:

> *[I]t is imperative for trustees to make their leadership gifts early to serve as an example for others. . . . [And,] Trustee leadership in recruiting workers, cultivating, [and] soliciting . . . is absolutely crucial . . .* (1977, p. 47).

Because "fund raising is the one major activity in which trustees step beyond their policy and oversight roles and become active players" (Pocock 1989, p. 23), the chief development officer often has more direct involvement with the trustees than any other officer with the possible exception of the president:

> *[M]uch of what the president should be doing [with the trustees] also applies to the development officer. The relationship with trustees in both cases must be extremely close. The development officer is a specialist and perhaps has more time to devote to this relationship than the president* (Franz 1981, p. 164).

Operationally, most writers see the development officer's relationship to the trustees in Catalyst or Manager terms. For example, Kinnison and Ferin define four responsibilities of development officers, three of which are clearly Catalyst or Manager functions and are described in terms characteristic of writers representing those schools:

1. *To raise and* enable *the trustees' and the president's participation in the fund-raising process by providing information, training, and preparatory work.*
2. *To provide an effective "teamwork" environment.*
3. *To translate mission, priority, and need into readily usable case statements and plans of action.*
4. *To be involved personally in the fund-raising process* (1989, p. 58, emphasis added).

Patton also uses the terminology of Catalyst and Manager:

The CDO [chief development officer] must manage *two complementary functions of development activity: creating materials and cultivating donors. . . . Above all, it is the CDO's responsibility to* facilitate *the trustees' and the president's participation in the fund-raising process* (1993, p. 55, emphasis added).

A few authors seem to view the development officer as an institutional Leader, in a position to influence, even shape the board of trustees. As Franz notes:

In institutions where the development officer has been employed for a relatively long period of time, it is not unusual for him or her to provide the closest link between the campus and the board (1981, p. 164).

Grace also sees the development staff in a leadership role with regard to the board, saying that "fund-raising leadership is modeled by staff members and transferred to the board through standards, performance, and example." This leadership responsibility is "reciprocal" and "a decline in leadership by either staff or board will lead to a subsequent decline in leadership by the other" (1991b, p. 169).

Most suggest that the development officer's influence with the board be maintained within appropriate boundaries. Franz, a development officer himself, suggests that the chief development officer should be alert to candidates for board membership but must "find an acceptable method to communicate his suggestions to the chairman of the board or the chairman of the nominating committee" (1981, p. 163).

Pocock, a trustee, maintains that "the chief development officer . . . should talk to the trustees more frequently and in greater depth than other administrative officers are allowed to" but that "such communications should be properly channeled and monitored" (1989, p. 23). As a university president addressing himself to development officers, Trachtenberg is direct on this point:

> *We are working together in some very sensitive projects with people, like trustees, who are crucial to the success of my presidency as well as the campus. I expect you to support me, warn me when you see trouble brewing, and cover me when I make a mistake* (1993, p. 19).

What Should Be the Development Officer's Role in Institutional Planning?

As discussed earlier, authors of the Leader category share an emphasis on the development officer's role as a professional and as a significant officer of the institution. This perception of the development officer's role raises the question of what his or her participation and influence should be in setting institutional policies and priorities.

In their 1990 review, Brittingham and Pezzullo find the literature clear and consistent on this point:

> *The literature on fund raising makes much of the point that fund raisers should not set their institution's priorities for fund raising: they should raise money for institutional priorities. . . . [T]he underlying reason for such seeming deference by the fund raiser is that each request for support for a particular purpose is a statement about what the institution would like to become (or remain) and that each request is a statement about how the institution would see itself and the world* (1990, p. 57).

Sharing that view, Kinnison and Ferin present a hypothetical situation in which a development officer has solicited a restricted gift for a purpose not covered in the institution's master plan. They suggest that the "chief development officer overstepped the boundary between his own role as facilitator and [the] role as designer of institutional mission and priorities." They further suggest that the president's response to this transgression "might involve termination of the development officer" (1989, p. 59).

However, some writers advocate a larger role for the development officer as an institutional leader involved in establishing institutional mission and priorities. After reviewing a number of development offices, Duronio and Loessin concluded that the development officer must be at the center of institutional planning.

> *In most business operations, the vice president for sales is a major participant in setting company direction, because the sales staff are most closely in touch with the market and what customers want. Similarly, in most . . . effective institutions, vice presidents and other senior development staff [play] an important role in helping to set institutional long-range goals and directions* (1991a, p. 132).

Rick Nahm and Robert Zemsky believe the successful development program is intertwined with institutional planning. Stating that higher education fund-raising is "at a crossroads," they identify three goals as essential:

> *fund raising must be: need-driven rather than donor-driven, capable of providing relief to the operating budget, and designed to integrate the institution's vision* (1993, p. 59).

To achieve these goals, the chief development officer must be viewed as an integral part of the institution's leadership, and the faculty and top nondevelopment administrators must take part in the development office's planning. This integration of the institution's priority needs with the development office's fund-raising plan results in a

> *concise list of gift opportunities which, when funded, will clearly advance the institutional plan. When fund-raising objectives are presented in this context, needs become opportunities and gifts become investments* (1993, p. 64).

Worth also advocates a leadership role for development officers within their institutions, arguing that

> *[T]he issues facing fund raising and philanthropy are so inseparable from those of higher education as a whole that*

*development officers must participate in the wider debate.
. . . We [development officers] have a greater opportunity
than ever before to join the larger discussion about the substantive higher education issues to which our own work is
inextricably related* (1993, p. 409).

There is, indeed, evidence that chief development officers
are playing such leadership roles. In his 1980 study, Coloia
found that 72 percent of development officers surveyed were
participants in institutional planning and concluded that

*The office charged with fund raising can no longer be con-
sidered an appendage to the administrative structure uti-
lized in decision making. The inclusion of the chief development officer into the highest administrative echelons gives
evidence to support the notion that fund raising is crucial
to institutional survival and that the chief development
officer is functioning in a peer relationship with other top
administrators* (1980, p. 272).

A more recent study (Duronio and Loessin 1991b) suggests
that the development officer's participation in institutional
planning had become even more common. All of the eight
development officers they studied were involved, to some
extent, in setting institutional priorities and fund-raising goals,
and serving as an institutional officer was a primary function
for four of them.

Who Should Solicit the Gift?

The question of who should actually solicit the gift could be
considered the ultimate "practical question" with regard to
the development officer's role. Consistent with their perspective, those who adhere to the Salesman approach argue that
gifts should be solicited by the development staff member.
McGannon states flatly,

*Volunteers serve many useful functions in fund raising,
but soliciting gifts isn't one of them. The most important
and dedicated operation in all our contact with major
donors belongs to the staff. . . . Major gifts are almost always*

the result of ongoing efforts by professional staff members who are better suited to make the ask (1992, p. 15).

Panas agrees, saying, "the chief executive officer of an institution *or a staff person* is most often the best person to get the gift" (1988, p. 221, emphasis added).

By definition, Catalysts believe that they are in a support role. Volunteers are critical, therefore, for raising the gifts. In Frantzreb's view,

> *Volunteers are the front line salesmen for the development officer. Trustees (authenticators) must lead the way, set the pace, set the tone, lead first and give first. Then other volunteers who are carefully selected, trained and conditioned to be salesmen for the institution carry the message and bring home the results under the tutelage and assistance of the development sales officer* (1970, p. 21).

Seymour's assessment of donor motivation is so well-known that it has become a cliche. He says that donors give "because people at their own or a higher level ask them to give" (1966, p. 29). He concludes,

> *Just as any good pair of scissors needs two blades, with each blade helping to keep the other sharp, so it is that any good fund-raising operation needs both kinds of leadership— the layman who leads and the staff man who manages and serves* (1966, p. 179).

Brakeley also believes the volunteer is crucial for the actual solicitation. In a sample job description outlining a director of development's duties, Brakeley does not include any solicitation responsibilities until far down the list, and then with significant caveats: "Prepare and, *when appropriate, assist in presenting* proposals and grant applications to prospective donors" (1980, p. 67, emphasis added).

Abbie von Schlegell sounds a Catalyst theme when she stresses that volunteers are essential: "Volunteers have influence. They can open doors that few staff members can move. . . . What's more, by having a peer make the approach, the institution demonstrates proper respect for the prospective donor" (1992, p. 21). Dove notes with dismay the decreasing role of volunteers: "Recent years have seen a trend toward professional staff filling the role of volunteers, particularly in the cultivation and solicitation of major prospects. This is a great mistake" (1988, p. 166).

Those in the Manager category often share with the Catalysts the belief that their role is to stay behind the scenes when it comes to solicitation. Greenfield, for example, writes,

Every fund-raising activity has an absolute need for volunteer leadership. Without someone to recruit others, to conduct the meetings, to provide direction (and respect), to keep the program on track, and to insist on performance and success, the entire effort is lost (1991, p. 87).

Broce admits that at times the staff member may be unable to avoid soliciting, but, "the volunteer is critically important in serious fund-raising efforts. Without the support and commitment of volunteers, most programs erode into mere donation-gathering activities" (1979, p. 183). Wireman agrees:

Development officers and presidents cannot alone raise money; they must have strong trustee and alumni support. Only to the degree that an institution has a strong president and development staff to mobilize the trustees, alumni and friends to work will the institution sustain an effective development effort (Boling et al. 1981, p. 355).

Those who define the Leader category are split on the issue of who is the proper solicitor. Some authors who generally advocate a Leader role agree with the Salesmen that the staff are better solicitors. James Frick, for example, believes that "an important principle of fund raising is continuity of contact with the prospect of [sic] benefactor. It is very important that the principal contact with a prospect be the same person so that a bond of friendship is established between them" ("Capsules of Advice" 1981, p. 373). Frick warns that this bond can only be established and maintained by a staff member:

Of course, in multiyear capital campaigns, development contact at somewhat modest levels of giving must be assigned to volunteers. By and large, however, and particularly in the leadership gift areas, I contend that development work for a college or university is for those whose lives have been committed to the work of education and its

More commonly, development officers are transitory, while volunteers provide long-term continuity.

advancement. . . . [W]hatever success I have enjoyed in advancement work has been based largely on large-gift solicitation by those people closest to the epicenter of the institution (1986, p. 366).

It should be noted, however, that Frick's perspective is unusual. He was, for many years, a very influential development officer and university figure at Notre Dame. In fact, he personified the university in the eyes of many, as he established and maintained the bonds to which he refers above. More commonly, however, development officers are transitory, while volunteers provide long-term continuity. Therefore, most writers who call for the Leader approach advocate a significant role for volunteers. Payton and his colleagues, for example, state,

> *Volunteers are essential to the voluntary tradition, and we decry the tendency for professional fund raisers to displace them. . . . We believe that voluntary service is the life-blood of philanthropy. Volunteers are an essential but diminishing force. The denigration of the role of volunteers by professionals and other staff may be weakening the general public's will to volunteer. Volunteers are philanthropy's most credible voice; they legitimate the voice of the professional* (1991a, pp. 15+).

David Dunlop adds another reason for using volunteers to solicit gifts: It is an excellent strategy to involve the volunteer in the life of the institution. While stating that "an institution may find it easy or efficient to use its development staff to solicit gifts," Dunlop argues against the practice because "doing so means discarding priceless opportunities to involve regular and special gift prospects" (1993, p. 101). Dunlop's definition of "volunteer" is broad, however, including "faculty, trustees, students, neighbors, classmates, officers of your institution, staff—almost anyone who knows and cares about both the prospect and the institution" (1993, p. 108).

In general, then, the Salesmen define their role as being the direct solicitor. Catalysts and Managers believe volunteers should fulfill this role, while the development officer remains behind the scenes. The Leader category is split on this issue, perhaps reflecting the fact that they assume the development officer occupies a position of considerable influence in the institution. Therefore, some have concluded that they are better able to solicit gifts, but most continue to rely upon the volunteer tradition. In the words of these authors, "fund raising is too important to be left entirely to fund raisers" (Payton, Rosso, and Tempel 1991b, p. 5).

Summary

This section has considered four practical questions discussed in the development literature. As expected, authors' answers to these questions reflect their positions in the Salesman, Catalyst, Manager, or Leader categories.

While authors of the Salesman category view the development officer as a "lone wolf" who solicits gifts, writers of the other categories discuss the development officer, president, and trustees as a fund-raising team and emphasize the "three-party relationship" among them.

Most presidents who have addressed the subject see themselves as the chief fund-raisers for their institutions and the development officer in a supportive role as Catalyst or Manager. In this conception, the relationship between the development officer and the president is essential to success. Personal chemistry and a common understanding of roles are mentioned as ingredients of a good relationship.

Most writers see the leadership and involvement of trustees as essential to successful fund-raising. Most writers view the development officer as acting in a Catalyst or Manager role with regard to the trustees. Because trustees go beyond policy-making roles to actively participate in fund-raising, the development officer is often closer to them than any other institutional officer except the president. But, the development officer must keep communication with trustees within appropriate boundaries in order to preserve his or her relationship with the president.

The literature is divided on the appropriate role of the development officer in institutional planning. The Catalyst and Manager viewpoints hold that the development officer's job is to raise funds for institutional and academic priorities determined by others, including the president, faculty, and trustees. Others see the development officer in a Leader role, as an institutional officer at the center of planning and with a voice in determining institutional missions and goals. Some recent studies indicate that the majority of chief development officers are involved in institutional planning, to some degree.

The question of who should solicit gifts is the ultimate "practical question." Predictably, writers of the Salesman school argue that development staff members are best able to represent the institution to donors. Authors of the Catalyst and Manager approach emphasize the need for volunteer solicitations, organized and supported by the development officer. Authors of the Leader category are divided on the question, with some arguing that the chief development officer should be a principal spokesperson for the institution while others see the volunteer's role in solicitation as preferred.

CONCLUSIONS AND RECOMMENDATIONS

Development officers have one of the most difficult jobs on any campus. Their results are measurable and visible, but not fully within their control. The campus budget officer is also measured by results, but at least half of the equation—expenditures—is arguably within his or her control. Development officers are measured by the amount of revenue they produce and that depends largely on variables over which they have no influence, such as alumni sentiment and the local or national economy.

In the view of most authorities, fund-raising success is the result of a team effort, related to the effectiveness and commitment of the president and trustees as well as the development officer. It is the development officer's career that is most closely tied to this success, yet he or she has little ability to determine who the other players will be or how they will perform.

Like development officers, enrollment management officers are required to meet measurable goals, and the revenue implications of their work are even more vital to their institutions. But, admissions recruiters are at least working with "prospects," i.e., potential students, who have already made the initial decision to attend college. The goal is to persuade them to attend a specific college. Fund-raising is an even more difficult assignment, since it requires a "double sell"—persuading the donor to give at all and then to give to the specific institution (Trachtenberg 1991).

Development officers share with only a few others—including the president, the trustees, and perhaps the chief financial officer—the responsibility to concern themselves with the welfare of the institution as a whole and to work toward assuring its strength in the future as well as the present. This perspective sometimes can be at odds with the priorities—and demands—of others whose horizons are more parochial and immediate. This may include deans or department heads within a university and even presidents and boards of institutions facing immediate financial pressures.

The inherent difficulty of the development officer's role is compounded by differing perceptions of its definition. This could account, at least in part, for the high turnover of incumbents and the isolation of development officers from the academic communities they serve. And it is reasonable to believe that these conditions negatively affect the performance of development officers and limit their effectiveness in serving their institutions.

This situation reflects the historical evolution of the field, as outlined earlier in this report, and development's relative youth as a definable occupation or "profession." The earliest "development officers" were Salesmen—that is, solitary figures who solicited gifts without the trappings of a large or specialized development "operation" as exists today at many institutions. Later came the consultants such as Ward—Catalysts who did not solicit funds but who guided a fund-raising "process." Only within the last 40 years have development officers become common as full-time members of college and university staffs, and their visible presence at many public institutions is an even more recent phenomenon. The significant growth of development staffs and budgets in the 1980s, at all types of institutions, has expanded the Manager role, but that new responsibility is not fully recognized by some observers. The rise of the chief development officer as an institutional Leader is a very recent phenomenon. Its reality has not been fully recognized nor its implications for institutions adequately considered.

Perception often lags reality. It is understandable that some views of the development officer's role in higher education seem stuck in the reality of an earlier era that was, after all, not that very long ago. In this report, we have attempted to bring some structure to thinking about the development officer's role by defining the four schools of thought—Salesman, Catalyst, Manager, or Leader—and by placing major authors among them depending upon which of the four development roles they emphasize. And, we have proposed a "development officer paradigm" to illustrate how the four roles relate to each other within the context of an individual development career and within the organization of a development office. We hope this paradigm may provide a useful tool for analyzing both development and the literature concerning it, but we recognize and acknowledge that it offers only a start. There is a need for additional research and discussion as a basis for development's advancement as a "profession" and its more effective service to higher education.

What Is and What Should Be?

There is a tension in the literature between what is and what should be. Arguing that gifts *should* be solicited by volunteers ignores the fact that many are, in fact, solicited by development staff. Observing the fact that development officers *do* have a say in setting institutional goals and priorities is not the same as arguing that this is desirable.

Much of the practitioner literature is written from a "should-be" perspective. An increasing number of studies have attempted to identify the characteristics of successful institutions and fund-raising programs. However, there is a scant literature concerning what development officers actually do. There is a need for studies concerning how development officers allocate their time and talents among their various roles—in the course of a typical work day or week and over the course of a development career—and how this differs among various development positions and specialties. Of particular interest is the position of chief development officer and the question of how the four principal roles are reflected in this individual's activities.

With more information about the actual work performed by individuals in various development positions, it could be possible to create some standard, generic "job descriptions," including perhaps some definition of the traits and experiences required for success in each of them. Such information could be helpful to individuals in planning their development careers as well as to institutions in identifying appropriate candidates for development jobs.

Institutional Differences

As discussed above, development's youth as a profession and its history as a field account in part for its divergent images. This is compounded, however, by the diversity of higher education institutions. For example, roles are more specialized in large staffs at major universities and less so in one-person shops. A development officer may "look" very different in doing his or her job depending on the size and type of the institution he or she serves.

The development role may differ as well according to the traditions of the institution. For example, older private colleges with strong traditions of alumni voluntarism may call for the development staff to play a Catalyst role. Public universities, community colleges, and private urban universities, with less of a tradition of volunteer participation in fund-raising, may require that the development officer play the Salesman role to a greater extent.

There is, again, the tension between what is and what

should be. Some argue that volunteer leadership and participation in fund-raising is essential to success, while others argue that solicitations by staff are inherently preferable. Whichever view is accepted, some development officers will face institutional traditions inhospitable to the ideal and need to adapt.

For example, development officers who find unwilling alumni and trustee volunteers will have the choice either of becoming Salesmen or seeking other jobs. Those who work in a tradition of strong volunteer involvement may need to moderate any Salesman instincts to provide the kind of support their volunteer leaders expect. Indeed, the ability to adapt to institutional characteristics and traditions rather than adhere zealously to some ideal of fund-raising theory may be one of the most important characteristics of successful development officers. Studies of the development officer role across different types of institutions thus would provide important and practical additions to the literature.

The Fund-Raising Team

There is a need for more research and discussion of the development officer's relationship with the president and the trustees—particularly with the president, which the vast majority of authors say is vitally important. As this report has noted, most presidents who have written on the subject view the development officer role in Catalyst or Manager terms. However, presidents have undoubtedly read the literature with regard to what their roles in fund-raising should be and their published remarks may sometimes reflect that understanding rather than their true individual preferences or behavior. It may be that development officers must "tilt" toward one role or another to compensate for the varied talents and styles of their presidents.

Presidents who enjoy fund-raising and eagerly take the lead in soliciting gifts may require a development officer who is strong on inside management and staff support. Presidents who relish fund-raising less may need a development officer who spends most time outside making fund-raising calls, perhaps bringing the president in only at the final stage to close the gift. No matter what the literature may say about what the president's fund-raising role should be, the reality is that not all will be able or willing to exemplify that ideal. And no matter what the development officer may believe his or her role should be, he or she may need to adjust to the president's own strengths, weaknesses, and preferences in that regard. The alternative to such flexibility may be a continuing quest for the ideal and a series of unsuccessful appointments.

The Council for Advancement and Support of Education has held forums for development officers and presidents at which their critical relationship has been discussed. Perhaps through more such discussion some type of scale or typology could be developed along which presidents and development officers could rate their perceptions and preferences with regard to each others' role. Such ratings could be used as guides in making better matches (Trachtenberg 1991). At a minimum, presidents and development officers should openly discuss these issues in pre-employment interviews and periodically throughout their working relationship.

Development officers considering new positions might do well to analyze the situation in terms of the four development roles identified in this report. The title may be "vice president for development" or "director of development," but candidates might ask, "What, exactly, is the job?" Most position announcements and advertisements are vague in this regard, reading somewhat like the following:

> *The vice president for development is the chief fund-raising officer of Siwash College, responsible for the planning and direction of programs for annual and capital support. The vice president will manage professional and support staff of the development office, cultivate and solicit major gift prospects, and work closely with the president and volunteers in the college's upcoming campaign.*

This hypothetical description is typical of many that appear in the *Chronicle of Higher Education* and elsewhere. It suggests all four of the development officer roles: the Salesman (cultivate and solicit major gift prospects); the Catalyst (work closely with the president and volunteers); the Manager (manage professional and support staff); and the Leader (chief fund-raising officer [of the college]). It says everything—and therefore nothing—about the relative emphasis on the four roles that the situation and players at Siwash College will expect and require in practice.

The Development Officer's Role in the Future

As discussed previously, the development officer's current role has evolved historically with changes in society and higher education itself. It is interesting to speculate how today's trends may alter it in the future.

If, as some observers argue, there is a decline in voluntarism throughout our society, will development officers be forced into more and more direct solicitation? If so, and if those who say that a team approach is essential are correct, will development officers possibly be able to meet the needs of their institutions and the expectations placed upon them?

What are the implications of the increasing emphasis on planned giving? Will the technical expertise required in arranging planned gifts lead to more solicitation of gifts by development staff? Will the development officer be able to win support for the program from boards and presidents if an increasing number of gifts are available only in the long term, perhaps beyond the tenure of current incumbents?

Increasing government regulation of fund-raising and the growing sophistication of development information systems are creating a growing cadre of back-office development managers and an identifiable new subspecialty of the profession, known as "development services," has already emerged. Will this trend lead to divisions and tensions within the development profession itself between staff who are internally and externally oriented? Will the management of the development operation ultimately become too technical and complex to be managed by top development officers, most of whom pursued their careers on the "external vector?" If so, will development services eventually be combined with other administrative operations of the institution under vice presidents for business or finance, thus reducing the development officer's Manager role?

Remembering that fund-raising and philanthropy have been part of American colleges and universities from the beginning, and it seems likely that the development officer role is one likely to survive. It is equally likely that it will continue to change in response to the evolving needs of institutions and with the circumstances of higher education itself.

REFERENCES

The Educational Resources Information Center (ERIC) Clearinghouse on Higher Education abstracts and indexes the current literature on higher education for inclusion in ERIC's data base and announcement in ERIC's monthly bibliographic journal, *Resources in Education* (RIE). Most of these publications are available through the ERIC Document Reproduction Service (EDRS). For publications cited in this bibliography that are available from EDRS, ordering number and price code are included. Readers who wish to order a publication should write to the ERIC Document Reproduction Service, 7420 Fullerton Rd., Suite 110, Springfield, VA 22153-2852. (Phone orders with VISA or MasterCard are taken at 800-443-ERIC or 703-440-1400.) When ordering, please specify the document (ED) number. Documents are available as noted in microfiche (MF) and paper copy (PC). If you have the price code ready when you call EDRS, an exact price can be quoted. The last page of the latest issue of *Resources in Education* also has the current cost, listed by code.

Berendt, R.J., and J.R. Taft. 1983. *How to Rate Your Development Office: A Fund-Raising Primer for the Chief Executive*. Washington, D.C.: Taft Corporation.

Bloland, H.G., and R. Bornstein. 1991. "Fund Raising in Transition: Strategies to Professionalization." In *Taking Fund Raising Seriously: Advancing the Profession and Practice of Raising Money*, edited by D.F. Burlingame and L.J. Hulse. San Francisco: Jossey-Bass.

Blumenstyk, G. May 11, 1994. "Harvard's Brass Ring." *The Chronicle of Higher Education*: A35-A36.

Boling et al. 1981. "College Presidents' Perspectives on Development." In *Handbook for Educational Fund Raising*, edited by F.C. Pray. San Francisco: Jossey-Bass.

Brakeley Jr., G.A. 1980. *Tested Ways to Successful Fund Raising*. New York: AMACOM.

Brittingham, B.E., and T.R. Pezzullo. 1990. *Campus Green: Fund Raising in Higher Education*. ASHE-ERIC Higher Education Report No. 1. Washington, D.C.: School of Education and Human Development, The George Washington University. ED 321 706. 146 pp. MF-01; PC-06.

Broce, T.E. 1979. *Fund Raising: The Guide to Raising Money from Private Sources*. Norman: University of Oklahoma Press.

Buchanan, P.M. 1993. Educational Fund Raising as a Profession. In *Educational Fund Raising: Principles and Practice*, edited by M.J. Worth. Phoenix: Oryx Press/American Council on Education.

"Capsules of Advice Drawn From Experiences of Professionals." 1981. In *Handbook for Educational Fund Raising*, edited by F.C. Pray. San Francisco: Jossey-Bass.

Carbone, R.F. 1989. *Fund Raising as a Profession*. College Park, Md.: Clearinghouse for Research on Fund Raising.

Carroll, A. 1991. "My Sixteen Rules for a Successful Volunteer-Based Capital Campaign." In *Taking Fund Raising Seriously: Advancing the Profession and Practice of Raising Money*, edited by D.F. Burlingame and L.J. Hulse. San Francisco: Jossey-Bass.

Coloia Jr., L.S. 1980. "Fund Raising in Private Higher Education: An Analysis of the Role of the Development Officer as Administrator at Selected Institutions." Doctoral dissertation, Loyola University of Chicago.

Council for Advancement and Support of Education. 1994. *1994 CASE Members' Directory.* Washington, D.C.: Council for Advancement and Support of Education.

Council for the Advancement of Small Colleges, ed. 1970. *Development: A Team Approach.* Washington, D.C.: Council for the Advancement of Small Colleges.

Council for Aid to Education. 1990. *Voluntary Support of Education 1988-89.* New York: Council for Aid to Education.

———. 1994. *Voluntary Support of Education, 1993.* New York: Council for Aid to Education.

Cutlip, S.M. 1965. *Fund Raising in the United States: Its Role in American Philanthropy.* New Brunswick, N.J.: Rutgers University Press.

Dove, K.E. 1988. *Conducting a Successful Capital Campaign: A Comprehensive Guide for Nonprofit Organizations.* San Francisco: Jossey-Bass.

Dunlop, D.R. 1993. "Major Gift Programs." In *Educational Fund Raising: Principles and Practice*, edited by M.J. Worth. Phoenix: Oryx Press/American Council on Education.

Duronio, M.A., and B.A. Loessin. 1991a. "Effective Business Practices in Fund Raising." In *Taking Fund Raising Seriously: Advancing the Profession and Practice of Raising Money*, edited by D.F. Burlingame and L.J. Hulse. San Francisco: Jossey-Bass.

———. 1991b. *Effective Fund Raising in Higher Education: Ten Success Stories.* San Francisco: Jossey-Bass.

Evans, G.A. 1986. "Organizing and Staffing the Development Office." In *Handbook of Institutional Advancement*, edited by A.W. Rowland. San Francisco: Jossey-Bass.

Fisher, J.L. 1989. *The President and Fund Raising.* New York: American Council on Education/Macmillan.

Fogal, R.E. 1991. "Standards and Ethics in Fund Raising." In *Achieving Excellence in Fund Raising: A Comprehensive Guide to Principles, Strategies, and Methods*, edited by H.A. Rosso. San Francisco: Jossey-Bass.

Franz, P.J. 1981. "Trustees Must Lead By Example." In *Handbook for Educational Fund Raising*, edited by F.C. Pray. San Francisco: Jossey-Bass.

Frantzreb, A.C. 1970. "The Development Function in the Seventies." In *Development: A Team Approach*, edited by The Council for the

Advancement of Small Colleges. Washington, D.C.: Council for the Advancement of Small Colleges.

———. 1991. "Seeking the Big Gift." In *Achieving Excellence in Fund Raising: A Comprehensive Guide to Principles, Strategies, and Methods*, edited by H.A. Rosso. San Francisco: Jossey-Bass.

Frick, J.W. 1981. "The Development Officer as Educator." In *Handbook for Educational Fund Raising*, edited by F.C. Pray. San Francisco: Jossey-Bass.

———. 1986. "Educational Philanthropy: A Perspective of Three Decades." In *Handbook of Institutional Advancement*, edited by A.W. Rowland. San Francisco: Jossey-Bass.

Grace, K.S. 1991a. "Managing for Results." In *Achieving Excellence in Fund Raising: A Comprehensive Guide to Principles, Strategies, and Methods*, edited by H.A. Rosso. San Francisco: Jossey-Bass.

———. 1991b. "Leadership and Team Building." In *Achieving Excellence in Fund Raising: A Comprehensive Guide to Principles, Strategies, and Methods*, edited by H.A. Rosso. San Francisco: Jossey-Bass.

Greenfield, J.M. 1991. *Fund Raising: Evaluating and Managing the Fund Development Process*. New York: John Wiley & Sons, Inc.

Harrah-Conforth, J., and J. Borsos. 1991. "The Evolution of Professional Fund Raising: 1890-1990." In *Taking Fund Raising Seriously: Advancing the Profession and Practice of Raising Money*, edited by D.F. Burlingame and L.J. Hulse. San Francisco: Jossey-Bass.

Kelly, K.S. 1991. *Fund Raising and Public Relations: A Critical Analysis*. Hillsdale, N.J.: Lawrence Erlbaum Associates, Inc.

Kinnison, W.A., and M.J. Ferin. 1989. "The Three-Party Relationship." In *Fund Raising Leadership: A Guide for College and University Boards*, edited by J.W. Pocock. Washington, D.C.: Association of Governing Boards of Universities and Colleges.

Koile, E.A., and W. Gould. 1981. "Careful Listening as the Revealing Art of Development. In *Handbook for Educational Fund Raising*, edited by F.C. Pray. San Francisco: Jossey-Bass.

Lawson, C.E. Winter 1990. "The Nineties: Worrisome Trends in Fund Raising." *The Journal* (National Society of Fund Raising Executives): 9-12.

McGannon, J.B. January 1992. "Who Should Ask for the Gift? The Staff." *CASE Currents*: 14-18.

McGoldrick, W.P. 1993. "Campaigning in the Nineties." In *Educational Fund Raising: Principles and Practice*, edited by M.J. Worth. Phoenix: Oryx Press/American Council on Education.

Muller, S. 1986. "The Definition and Philosophy of Institutional Advancement." In *Handbook of Institutional Advancement*, edited by A.W. Rowland. San Francisco: Jossey-Bass.

Murray, D.J. 1987. *The Guaranteed Fund-Raising System: A Systems Approach to Planning and Controlling Fund Raising*. Boston:

American Institute of Management.

Nahm, R., and R.M. Zemsky. 1993. The Role of Institutional Planning in Fund Raising. In *Educational Fund Raising: Principles and Practice*, edited by M.J. Worth. Phoenix: Oryx Press/American Council on Education.

Osborne, K.E. 1993. "Hiring, Training, and Retaining Development Staff." In *Educational Fund Raising: Principles and Practice*, edited by M.J. Worth. Phoenix: Oryx Press/American Council on Education.

Panas, J. 1988. *Born to Raise: What Makes a Great Fundraiser, What Makes a Fundraiser Great*. Chicago: Pluribus Press.

———. 1984. *Mega Gifts: Who Gives Them, Who Gets Them*. Chicago: Pluribus Press.

Patton, S.L. 1993. "The Roles of Key Individuals." In *Educational Fund Raising: Principles and Practice*, edited by M.J. Worth. Phoenix: Oryx Press/American Council on Education.

Payton, R.L. 1981. "Essential Qualities of the Development Officer." In *Handbook for Educational Fund Raising*, edited by F.C. Pray. San Francisco: Jossey-Bass.

———. 1989. "The Ethics and Values of Fund Raising." In *The President and Fund Raising*, edited by J.L. Fisher and G.H. Quehl. New York: American Council on Education/Macmillan.

Payton, R.L., H.A. Rosso, and E.R. Tempel. 1991a. "Taking Fund Raising Seriously: An Agenda." In *Taking Fund Raising Seriously: Advancing the Profession and Practice of Raising Money,* edited by D.F. Burlingame and L.J. Hulse. San Francisco: Jossey-Bass.

———. 1991b. "Toward a Philosophy of Fund Raising." In *Taking Fund Raising Seriously: Advancing the Profession and Practice of Raising Money,* edited by D.F. Burlingame and L.J. Hulse. San Francisco: Jossey-Bass.

Pendleton, N. 1981. *Fund Raising: A Guide for Non-Profit Organizations*. Englewood Cliffs, N.J.: Prentice-Hall, Inc.

Pocock, J.W., ed. 1989. *Fund-Raising Leadership: A Guide for College and University Boards*. Washington, D.C.: Association of Governing Boards of Universities and Colleges.

Pray, F.C., ed. 1981. *Handbook for Educational Fund Raising*. San Francisco: Jossey-Bass.

Reilly, T.A., ed. 1985. *Raising Money Through an Institutionally-related Foundation*. Washington, D.C.: Council for Advancement and Support of Education. ED 256 198. 91 pp. MF-01; PC-04.

Rosso, H.A., ed. 1991. *Achieving Excellence in Fund Raising: A Comprehensive Guide to Principles, Strategies, and Methods*. San Francisco: Jossey-Bass.

Schrum, J.B. 1993. "Ethical Issues in Fund Raising." In *Educational Fund Raising: Principles and Practice,* edited by M.J. Worth. Phoenix: Oryx Press/American Council on Education.

Seymour, H.J. 1966. *Designs for Fund-Raising: Principles, Patterns, Techniques.* New York: McGraw-Hill.

Stuhr, R.L., ed. 1977. *On Development.* Chicago: Gonser Gerber Tinker Stuhr.

Tempel, E.R. 1991. "Assessing Organizational Strengths and Vulnerabilities." In *Achieving Excellence in Fund Raising: A Comprehensive Guide to Principles, Strategies, and Methods,* edited by H.A. Rosso. San Francisco: Jossey-Bass.

Thomas, E.G. October 1987. "Flight Records: A Currents Study Confirms Advancement's Reputation for High Turnover." *CASE Currents:* 9-12.

Trachtenberg, S.J. 1991. Paper read at Council for Advancement and Support of Education Forum for Presidents and Chief Development Officers, Washington, D.C.

―――. November/December 1993. "What I Expect of My CDO." *CASE Currents:* 19-22.

Turner, R.C. 1991. "Metaphors Fund Raisers Live By: Language and Reality in Fund Raising." In *Taking Fund Raising Seriously: Advancing the Profession and Practice of Raising Money,* edited by D.F. Burlingame and L.J. Hulse. San Francisco: Jossey-Bass.

Upton, R.M. 1970. "Leadership for the Development Program." In *Development: A Team Approach,* edited by the Council for the Advancement of Small Colleges. Washington, D.C.: Council for the Advancement of Small Colleges.

von Schlegell, A.J. January 1992. "Who Should Ask for the Gift? Volunteers." *CASE Currents:* 21-23.

Worth, M.J. 1989. "The Institutionally-related Foundation in Public Colleges and Universities." In *Fund-raising Leadership: A Guide for College and University Boards,* edited by J.W. Pocock. Washington, D.C.: Association of Governing Boards of Universities and Colleges.

―――. 1993. *Educational Fund Raising: Principles and Practice.* Phoenix: Oryx Press/American Council on Education.

INDEX

A

alumni annual funds, 7
administrator, definition of, 28-29
American College Public Relations Association.
    See Council for Advancement and Support of Education
American Alumni Council.
    See Council for Advancement and Support of Education
anonymity, need for a passion for, 41

B

Beloit College, 54
Berendt and Taft (1983), 16, 41
Bloland and Bornstein (1991), 24, 46-47
Brakeley Jr., George (1980), 20, 43, 45, 62
Brittingham and Pezullo (1990), ix, 59
Broce, T. E. (1979), 21-22, 44, 45, 63
Buchanan (1993), 50-51

C

Carbone (1989), 48-49
career paths in development, 35-37
Carrol, Alex (1991), 23
Catalysts, role of development officer as, 19-22, 34
    emphasize fund-raising as a science, 43
    fund-raiser, 15-17, 19-21
    gift solicitation, in, 62-63
    relationship to trustees in terms of, 57-58
Cheshire, Richard (1981), 22-23
chief development officer, requirement of, 36-37
Coloia (1980), 61
Colton, Richard, 41
community colleges, most rapid growing fund-raising
   programs, 11
Council for Advancement and Support of Education, 9-11, 55, 71
Cutlip (1965), 12

D

Dartmouth College, 41
Dartmouth, early fund raising for, 7
Development Director
    lack of standard definition of role, 27
    position uncommon in 1949, 9
development
    equivalent to fund-raising, 4
    more professional term than fund-raising, 5-6
    origin of the term, 4
    "professional," 29

H

Harvard University,
  early fund raising for, 6, 7
  twentieth century growth in fund raising, 12
Hibbens, William, 6

I

Institutional
  advancement, definition of, 4
  development officer role in, 59-61
  staff and outside consultants, roles are distinct, 20

J

Johnson, John G., 23

K

Kalamazoo College, 53
Kansas University Endowment Association, 10-11
Kelly, Kathleen (1991), 20, 55
Ketchum, Carlton, 8
Ketchum, David (1981), 43-44
Ketchum, George, 8
Kinnison and Ferin (1989), 57, 59-60

L

Lawson, Charles, 13
Leader, development officer as, 15-17, 23-25, 58
  description of, 34-35
  large role for as, 60-61
  solicitation of gifts, in, 63-64
Lowe, Helen, xi

M

Manager, development officer as, 15-17, 21-23, 34
  emphasize fund-raising as a science, 43
  in solicitation of gifts, 63-64
  opposite of Salesman approach, 22
  relationship to trustees in terms of, 57-58
Marist College, 54
Marts, Arnaud, 8
McCord, Charles (1981), 39
McGannon, J. Barry (1992), 19, 61-62
McGoldrick (1993), 54
Muller, Steven (1986), 23
Murray, Dennis (1987), 43, 54

N

Northwestern University, 4

Nahm and Zemsky (1993), 60
Notre Dame University, 64
National Society of Fund-Raising Executives, 10

O
Osborne, Karen (1993), 17
outside consultants and institutional staff, roles are distinct, 20

P
Panas, Jerold
 (1984), 22
 (1988), 16, 18, 19, 39-42, 44, 62
Patton (1993), 58
Payton
 (1981), 40
 (1989), 6
 and colleagues (1991a), 23, 45-48, 64
Peter, Hugh, 6
philanthropy in practice, 6
Pierce, Lyman L., 7
Pocock (1989), 57, 59
Pray, Francis (1981), 10, 22, 24-25, 40
Princeton, early fund raising for, 7
profession, characteristics of a, 48-50
professionalization of development officers, disadvantages of, 51
Progressive Movement, 7

R
Rainsford, George N., 53-54
"Renaissance Man," need for, 39
resident manager, 9
Rosso, Henry (1991), 21, 45
Ryan, J. Patrick, 41

S
sales manager, development officer as a, 20
Salesman approach, development officer as 33-34
 as paid agent, 15, 17-19
 gift solicitation, 61-62, 64
 consistent advocates of, 40
 and Leaders, emphasize fund-raising as an art, 42
Schlegell, Abbie von (1992), 62
schools of thought on role of development officer, 2
Schrum, Jake (1993), 46
Seymour (1966), 18, 20, 44, 62
Stuhr (1977), 57

ASHE-ERIC HIGHER EDUCATION REPORTS

Since 1983, the Association for the Study of Higher Education (ASHE) and the Educational Resources Information Center (ERIC) Clearinghouse on Higher Education, a sponsored project of the School of Education and Human Development at The George Washington University, have cosponsored the *ASHE-ERIC Higher Education Report* series. The 1994 series is the twenty-third overall and the sixth to be published by the School of Education and Human Development at the George Washington University.

Each monograph is the definitive analysis of a tough higher education problem, based on thorough research of pertinent literature and institutional experiences. Topics are identified by a national survey. Noted practitioners and scholars are then commissioned to write the reports, with experts providing critical reviews of each manuscript before publication.

Eight monographs (10 before 1985) in the ASHE-ERIC Higher Education Report series are published each year and are available on individual and subscription bases. To order, use the order form on the last page of this book.

Qualified persons interested in writing a monograph for the ASHE-ERIC Higher Education Reports are invited to submit a proposal to the National Advisory Board. As the preeminent literature review and issue analysis series in higher education, we can guarantee wide dissemination and national exposure for accepted candidates. Execution of a monograph requires at least a minimal familiarity with the ERIC database, including *Resources in Education* and *Current Index to Journals in Education.* The objective of these Reports is to bridge conventional wisdom with practical research. Prospective authors are strongly encouraged to call Dr. Fife at 800-773-3742.

For further information, write to
    ASHE-ERIC Higher Education Reports
    The George Washington University
    1 Dupont Circle, Suite 630
    Washington, DC 20036
Or phone (202) 296-2597, toll-free: 800-773-ERIC.
    Write or call for a complete catalog.

ADVISORY BOARD

Barbara E. Brittingham
University of Rhode Island

Jay L. Chronister
University of Virginia

Rodolfo Z. Garcia
Michigan State University

Elizabeth M. Hawthorne
University of Toledo

Bruce Anthony Jones
University of Pittsburgh

L. Jackson Newell
University of Utah

Carolyn Thompson
State University of New York–Buffalo

CONSULTING EDITORS

Scott Rickard
Association of College Unions–International

G. Jeremiah Ryan
Harford Community College

Patricia A. Spencer
Riverside Community College

Frances Stage
Indiana University–Bloomington

Barbara E. Taylor
Association of Governing Boards

Carolyn J. Thompson
State University of New York–Buffalo

Sheila L. Weiner
Board of Overseers of Harvard College

Wesley K. Willmer
Biola University

Richard A. Yanikoski
De Paul University

REVIEW PANEL

Charles Adams
University of Massachusetts–Amherst

Louis Albert
American Association for Higher Education

Richard Alfred
University of Michigan

Henry Lee Allen
University of Rochester

Philip G. Altbach
Boston College

Marilyn J. Amey
University of Kansas

Kristine L. Anderson
Florida Atlantic University

Karen D. Arnold
Boston College

Robert J. Barak
Iowa State Board of Regents

Alan Bayer
Virginia Polytechnic Institute and State University

John P. Bean
Indiana University–Bloomington

John M. Braxton
Vanderbilt University

Ellen M. Brier
Tennessee State University

Barbara E. Brittingham
The University of Rhode Island

Dennis Brown
University of Kansas

Peter McE. Buchanan
Council for Advancement and
    Support of Education

Patricia Carter
University of Michigan

John A. Centra
Syracuse University

Arthur W. Chickering
George Mason University

Darrel A. Clowes
Virginia Polytechnic Institute and State University

Deborah M. DiCroce
Piedmont Virginia Community College

Cynthia S. Dickens
Mississippi State University

Sarah M. Dinham
University of Arizona

Kenneth A. Feldman
State University of New York–Stony Brook

Dorothy E. Finnegan
The College of William & Mary

Mildred Garcia
Montclair State College

Rodolfo Z. Garcia
Commission on Institutions of Higher Education

Kenneth C. Green
University of Southern California

James Hearn
University of Georgia

Edward R. Hines
Illinois State University

Deborah Hunter
University of Vermont

Philo A. Hutchison
Georgia State University

Bruce Anthony Jones
University of Pittsburgh

Elizabeth A. Jones
The Pennsylvania State University

Kathryn Kretchsmer
University of Kansas

Martha V. Krotseng
State College and University Systems of West Virginia

George D. Kuh
Indiana University–Bloomington

Daniel T. Layzell
University of Wisconsin System

Patrick G. Love
Kent State University

Cheryl D. Lovell
State Higher Education Executive Officers

Meredith Jane Ludwig
American Association of State Colleges and Universities

Dewayne Matthews
Western Interstate Commission for Higher Education

Mantha V. Mehallis
Florida Atlantic University

Toby Milton
Essex Community College

James R. Mingle
State Higher Education Executive Officers

John A. Muffo
Virginia Polytechnic Institute and State University

L. Jackson Newell
University of Utah

James C. Palmer
Illinois State University

Robert A. Rhoads
The Pennsylvania State University

G. Jeremiah Ryan
Harford Community College

Mary Ann Danowitz Sagaria
The Ohio State University

Daryl G. Smith
The Claremont Graduate School

Carolyn Thompson
State University of New York–Buffalo

William G. Tierney
University of Southern California

Susan B. Twombly
University of Kansas

Robert A. Wallhaus
University of Illinois–Chicago

Harold Wechsler
University of Rochester

Elizabeth J. Whitt
University of Illinois–Chicago

Michael J. Worth
The George Washington University

RECENT TITLES

1994 ASHE-ERIC Higher Education Reports

1. The Advisory Committee Advantage: Creating an Effective
   Strategy for Programmatic Improvement
   by Lee Teitel

2. Collaborative Peer Review: The Role of Faculty in Improving
   College Teaching
   by Larry Keig and Michael D. Waggoner

3. Prices, Productivity, and Investment: Assessing Financial Strategies in Higher Education
   by Edward P. St. John

1993 ASHE-ERIC Higher Education Reports

1. The Department Chair: New Roles, Responsibilities and
   Challenges
   Alan T. Seagren, John W. Creswell, and Daniel W. Wheeler

2. Sexual Harassment in Higher Education: From Conflict to
   Community
   Robert O. Riggs, Patricia H. Murrell, and JoAnn C. Cutting

3. Chicanos in Higher Education: Issues and Dilemmas for the
   21st Century
   by Adalberto Aguirre, Jr., and Ruben O. Martinez

4. Academic Freedom in American Higher Education: Rights,
   Responsibilities, and Limitations
   by Robert K. Poch

5. Making Sense of the Dollars: The Costs and Uses of Faculty
   Compensation
   by Kathryn M. Moore and Marilyn J. Amey

6. Enhancing Promotion, Tenure and Beyond: Faculty Socialization
   as a Cultural Process
   by William G. Tierney and Robert A. Rhoads

7. New Perspectives for Student Affairs Professionals: Evolving
   Realities, Responsibilities and Roles
   by Peter H. Garland and Thomas W. Grace

8. Turning Teaching Into Learning: The Role of Student Responsibility in the Collegiate Experience
   by Todd M. Davis and Patricia Hillman Murrell

1992 ASHE-ERIC Higher Education Reports

1. The Leadership Compass: Values and Ethics in Higher Education
   John R. Wilcox and Susan L. Ebbs

2. Preparing for a Global Community: Achieving an International Perspective in Higher Education
   Sarah M. Pickert

3. Quality: Transforming Postsecondary Education
   Ellen Earle Chaffee and Lawrence A. Sherr

4. Faculty Job Satisfaction: Women and Minorities in Peril
   Martha Wingard Tack and Carol Logan Patitu

5. Reconciling Rights and Responsibilities of Colleges and Students: Offensive Speech, Assembly, Drug Testing, and Safety
   Annette Gibbs

6. Creating Distinctiveness: Lessons from Uncommon Colleges and Universities
   Barbara K. Townsend, L. Jackson Newell, and Michael D. Wiese

7. Instituting Enduring Innovations: Achieving Continuity of Change in Higher Education
   Barbara K. Curry

8. Crossing Pedagogical Oceans: International Teaching Assistants in U.S. Undergraduate Education
   Rosslyn M. Smith, Patricia Byrd, Gayle L. Nelson, Ralph Pat Barrett, and Janet C. Constantinides

1991 ASHE-ERIC Higher Education Reports

1. Active Learning: Creating Excitement in the Classroom
   Charles C. Bonwell and James A. Eison

2. Realizing Gender Equality in Higher Education: The Need to Integrate Work/Family Issues
   Nancy Hensel

3. Academic Advising for Student Success: A System of Shared Responsibility
   Susan H. Frost

4. Cooperative Learning: Increasing College Faculty Instructional Productivity
   David W. Johnson, Roger T. Johnson, and Karl A. Smith

5. High School–College Partnerships: Conceptual Models, Programs, and Issues
   Arthur Richard Greenberg

6. Meeting the Mandate: Renewing the College and Departmental Curriculum
   William Toombs and William Tierney

7. Faculty Collaboration: Enhancing the Quality of Scholarship and Teaching
   Ann E. Austin and Roger G. Baldwin

8. Strategies and Consequences: Managing the Costs in Higher Education
   John S. Waggaman

1990 ASHE-ERIC Higher Education Reports

1. The Campus Green: Fund Raising in Higher Education
   Barbara E. Brittingham and Thomas R. Pezzullo

2. The Emeritus Professor: Old Rank - New Meaning
   James E. Mauch, Jack W. Birch, and Jack Matthews

3. "High Risk" Students in Higher Education: Future Trends
   Dionne J. Jones and Betty Collier Watson

4. Budgeting for Higher Education at the State Level: Enigma, Paradox, and Ritual
   Daniel T. Layzell and Jan W. Lyddon

5. Proprietary Schools: Programs, Policies, and Prospects
   John B. Lee and Jamie P. Merisotis

6. College Choice: Understanding Student Enrollment Behavior
   Michael B. Paulsen

7. Pursuing Diversity: Recruiting College Minority Students
   Barbara Astone and Elsa Nuñez-Wormack

8. Social Consciousness and Career Awareness: Emerging Link in Higher Education
   John S. Swift, Jr.

1989 ASHE-ERIC Higher Education Reports

1. Making Sense of Administrative Leadership: The 'L' Word in Higher Education
   Estela M. Bensimon, Anna Neumann, and Robert Birnbaum

2. Affirmative Rhetoric, Negative Action: African-American and Hispanic Faculty at Predominantly White Universities
   Valora Washington and William Harvey

3. Postsecondary Developmental Programs: A Traditional Agenda with New Imperatives
   Louise M. Tomlinson

4. The Old College Try: Balancing Athletics and Academics in Higher Education
   John R. Thelin and Lawrence L. Wiseman

5. The Challenge of Diversity: Involvement or Alienation in the Academy?
   Daryl G. Smith

6. Student Goals for College and Courses: A Missing Link in Assessing and Improving Academic Achievement
   Joan S. Stark, Kathleen M. Shaw, and Malcolm A. Lowther

7. The Student as Commuter: Developing a Comprehensive Institutional Response
   Barbara Jacoby

8. Renewing Civic Capacity: Preparing College Students for Service and Citizenship
   Suzanne W. Morse

1988 ASHE-ERIC Higher Education Reports

1. The Invisible Tapestry: Culture in American Colleges and Universities
   George D. Kuh and Elizabeth J. Whitt

2. Critical Thinking: Theory, Research, Practice, and Possibilities
   Joanne Gainen Kurfiss

3. Developing Academic Programs: The Climate for Innovation
   Daniel T. Seymour

4. Peer Teaching: To Teach is To Learn Twice
   Neal A. Whitman

5. Higher Education and State Governments: Renewed Partnership, Cooperation, or Competition?
   Edward R. Hines

6. Entrepreneurship and Higher Education: Lessons for Colleges, Universities, and Industry
   James S. Fairweather

7. Planning for Microcomputers in Higher Education: Strategies for the Next Generation
   Reynolds Ferrante, John Hayman, Mary Susan Carlson, and Harry Phillips

8. The Challenge for Research in Higher Education: Harmonizing Excellence and Utility
   Alan W. Lindsay and Ruth T. Neumann

*Out-of-print. Available through EDRS. Call 1-800-443-ERIC.

ORDER FORM

Quantity   **Amount**

_____ Please begin my subscription to the 1994 *ASHE-ERIC Higher Education Reports* at $98.00, 31% off the cover price, starting with Report 1, 1994. Includes shipping. _____

_____ Please send a complete set of the 1993 *ASHE-ERIC Higher Education Reports* at $98.00, 31% off the cover price. Please add shipping charge, below. _____

Individual reports are avilable at the following prices:
1993 and 1994, $18.00; 1988-1992, $17.00; 1980-1987, $15.00

SHIPPING CHARGES
For orders of more than 50 books, please call for shipping information.

Total Quantity:	1st three books	Ea. addl. book
U.S., 48 Contiguous States		
Ground:	$3.75	$0.15
2nd Day*:	8.25	1.10
Next Day*:	18.00	1.60
Alaska & Hawaii (2nd Day Only)*:	13.25	1.40

U.S. Territories and Foreign Countries: Please call for shipping information.
*Order will be shipped within 24 hours of request.
All prices shown on this form are subject to change.

PLEASE SEND ME THE FOLLOWING REPORTS:

Quantity	Report No.	Year	Title	Amount

Please check one of the following:

☐ Check enclosed, payable to GWU–ERIC.	**Subtotal:** [ ]
☐ Purchase order attached ($45.00 minimum).	**Shipping:** [ ]
☐ Charge my credit card indicated below:	**Total Due:** [ ]
☐ Visa ☐ MasterCard	

[ ][ ][ ][ ][ ][ ][ ][ ][ ][ ][ ][ ][ ][ ][ ][ ][ ][ ]

Expiration Date _____

Name _____

Title _____

Institution ·_____

Address _____

City _____ State _____ Zip _____

Phone _____ Fax _____ Telex _____

Signature _____ Date _____

SEND ALL ORDERS TO: ASHE-ERIC Higher Education Reports
The George Washington University
One Dupont Cir., Ste. 630, Washington, DC 20036-1183
Phone: (202) 296-2597 • Toll-free: 800-773-ERIC